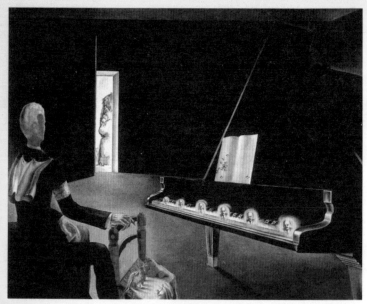

Salvador Dali: **Composition: Evocation of Lenin**

ANTI-COMMUNIST
MANIFESTO (1975)
FIRST ENGLISCH EDITION
© 2005 BY JIŘÍ KLOBOUK
TRANSLATION DANIEL MORGAN
EDITED BY SUSAN HALLETT

BERIA PRESS
Published in Canada
Contact adress: jiriklobouk@hotmail.com
ISBN 0-97338 77-0-X
PRINTED IN THE CZECH REPUBLIC BY QUALITY TOP S.R.O.

Jiří Klobouk

ANTI-COMMUNIST MANIFESTO

(1975)

A Period Document

*The period of reconciliation
between the free world and the
world of tyranny, which we are witnessing
at present, is one of the most tragic epoch in
the history of mankind. We state this with experienced
voices. We have lived with communism for endless
decades; we've been the witnesses and victims, the
observers and observed of each day of tyranny. These
are the days and lives of executioner butchers ruthlessly
practising their craft. How sad it is that this exquisite
world has to continue to suffer through the trials of the
endless terrors and hardships of war. What a pity our
testimony must be substantiated by further
barbarities of our common enemy.*

*America! Be brave tomorrow!
We wouldn't survive your humiliation and tears.*

Emigrants (1975).

TABLE OF CONTENTS:

PREFACE TO THE ENGLISH EDITION

The English edition of this document, written in Czech in Canada in 1975, was inspired by my recent visit to The Museum of Communism in Prague. The museum is a memorial to all victims of that totalitarian era - dead or alive - hundreds of millions of them.

I was astounded to encounter the sacred relics of the totalitarian regime on display for everyone to see: tools of socialist propaganda, statues of tyrants stripped to nakedness, slices of everyday life as empty as the bare grocery store shelves, fading flags, shiny medals and anti-American slogans in the most vitriolic of languages. The interrogator's room of the Secret Police (STB) envelops you with horror. You can hear the weak voice of your contemporary confessing after a sleepless night to a crime he or she didn't commit. You can almost smell the decomposing bodies of those who dared oppose the Big Red Lie.

For an unsuspecting spectator, an accidental tourist or the one who actually endured this nightmare, the exposition of things past is shattering. Many generations were subjected to tyranny of a proportion never experienced before or since. It is a great relief to enter the liberated streets of Prague. After all, not long ago, this part of the world was on a descending path of catastrophe - but then, one day the miracle happened.

I spent twenty years (between 1948 and 1968) in a "proletarian paradise". The last thing I expected to see during my lifetime was the fall of communism. It finally unraveled with domino-like effect in 1989. The sudden turn of events can be attributed to a number of factors listed here in chronological order:

1) Jazz music and its branching out in different directions from pop to rock. This music carried the seeds of freedom which rooted in the hearts and minds of youth everywhere.

2) The computer (communication) age which made it possible for uncensored information to cross international borders.

3) Lech Walesa, the Polish labour leader who challenged his communist masters with an iron will at the beginning of the 1980's. Pope John Paul II's blessing broadened his base of supporters.

4) President Ronald Reagan, a visionary of the earth's strongest democracy, who followed his words with deeds.

5) The strange appearance (and disappearance) of Mikhail Gorbachov on the Soviet Union's political scene. At that time no one expected that a party member indoctrinated by the state's morbid ideology would propose the demise of a system of which he himself was an inseparable part.

6) As a result of all the above, an ideological, economic and military surrender of The Union of Soviet Socialistic Republics has occurred. It was the surrender of a country which had inflicted nothing but misery on humankind for most of the 20th Century.

The aim of this book is to remind us that justice has yet to be done. The march of fascism and communism, the two most genocidal political systems of the past century, came to an abrupt end. The post Second World War order gave us assurance that Hitler's followers would never get another chance.

But up to this date, the new Russian state has not expressed regret. The most gruesome period in the history of man , which lasted 72 years, must never be forgotten. We must persevere, day and night, tirelessly and decisively, in requesting that Stalin's children denounce the crimes of their blood-soaked predecessors.

Finally, I have one more reason to resurrect this book in an English translation: when American writer Francis Fukuyama proclaimed the fall of communism to be the end of history, a new chapter of history had just begun - the rise of Islamic religious fanaticism. The events of September 11, 2001 made us realize the challenges ahead for the survival of civilization. This time our adversary is not Hitler or Stalin-like dictators but the omnipotent God of al-Qaeda-backed Islamic terrorists. To get rid of this God in the twisted minds and crippled souls of suicidal zealots is now the task of Sisyphus. When afterdeath becomes the prime objective of one's existence, life itself is meaningless. Communists (terrorist cells) had firmly established themselves in practically every corner of the world by 1975; Islamists (terrorist cells) are similarly established amongst us today. Reasoning will do nothing to stop them. Only our resolve will.

JK

Ottawa, Canada, May 2005

INTRODUCTION TO THE CZECH EDITION

There are writers and then there are writers. The latter group includes *Albert Camus*. I've been driving around with his *The Myth of Sisyphus* in the car for nearly 30 years. I can still vividly recall a certain spring day in 1969: I was visiting my cousin in New York, and it was there, among his books, that I found Camus' collection of essays. Having lived abroad for only a year, my English was still flawed, but this didn't stop me from having a go at a few pages of his *Message from Elsewhere*. It took just a few lines for him to captivate me. I submerged myself in this newly discovered world like a diver enshrouded in the secrecy of the dark depths of the sea. Fearing that I would be stripped of this rarest of pearls before I even had a chance to unveil its secrecy (and leave this veil to the mercy of the wind), I hid it early one morning in the narrow gap between the front seats of the car. Thus I spirited Camus away to Canada – as if he were my silent collaborator. The book remains wedged between the car seats. I still haven't finished it. (I've never been able to rid myself of the habit of only reading passages of my favorite writers). Whenever I find myself sitting inertly behind the wheel (picture me driving a member of the family to the dry cleaners to pick up a coat, and that person can't find the slip), I drift off into another world immersed in its pages. As the years rolled by and the worn-out cars were replaced by those a tad more drivable, I always remembered to transfer my Albert Camus to the place between the two slightly newer seats. As the cover and book itself began to fall apart and the pages began to yellow, there was nothing left for me to do but to get a new edition. This copy, with a boulder on the cover, glistened in its newness. When I compare the new and old copies, they remind me of two faces: the one newly born and the other slowly dying. But the soul within both is immortal. Albert Camus died in a car accident in 1960.

His essays in *The Myth of Sisyphus* are a placid analysis of the state of humanity's external and internal worlds: the desire to live. Each sentence is weather-beaten by Mediterranean Sea squalls. A warmth from the sands of Algeria emanates from each paragraph. The wandering moon casts a pale light over Oran. They were written at a time when the world offered hope that it would survive the wounds suffered from falling off a derailed train. When fascism came to an end people thought that once and for all after its horrors common sense would rule, and the destructive power in men would never again find fertile ground

– soil full of manure and worms where human beings, often with a masochistic perversity, sees to their own rotting.

***

This was written in 1975. Though calling something absurd is more or less the same as calling it preposterous, I'm having a hard time choosing which expression to use: We (we the parents and our grown children) were in Ottawa, Canada contemplating where to emigrate to for the second time. A mere seven years had passed since our first emigration from communist Czechoslovakia. The Vietnam War had ended in a debacle of the free world. Some 60,000 American soldiers lost their lives there. Everywhere else in the world, in Europe, in Africa and South America, new-age saviors took control of countries with breathtaking ease. Domestic collaboration in these countries came in the form of pinko prostitutes overeager to provide their services. Communist emissaries kept showing up at the doors of our Canadian homes promising paradise on earth as part of election campaigns. With an arrogance all their own, they predicted that the future was theirs for the taking. It was a time that filled us with a new dark anxiety. The free world was receding from a persistent tyrant up to the very edge of a bottomless abyss.

If the volcano should someday explode from its pent-up natural forces, this text is a result of my frustration in the benevolence of the then, hitherto free world, which refused to acknowledge the threat it faced in its entirety and depth.

Perhaps this is why this "literary proclamation" – *Anti-Communist Manifesto* – belongs among those "uncompromising" texts. It describes humanity's crossroads in which one road leads to hell and the other out of hell. Nothing in between. It's like a piano's black and white keys: The truth is white, and lies are black. Nothing in between. Nothing good can be said of a criminal who has killed his own family. And you can't award a medal for bravery to a man who saved his neighbor from a burning house, if he was the one to light the fire in the first place.

Written in 1975, this text is undoubtedly a reaction to the naivety, even puerility of people who saw the world at that time through rose-colored glasses. Even though the lives of all of us who personally experienced it clearly proved to what end a peaceful cooperation with the communists would lead, it was met with a shrug. They continued to deal with their archenemy as an equal. They assured him that he had the same right to exist as they. And if a solitary voice of dissent was heard against this red terror spreading slowly but surely over the world, it was quickly silenced. It was then explained to the enemy that these were merely the voices of extremists.

The expression anti-communist and its relevant derivatives

have become taboo in the Western press and mass media. Torpidity and lethargy have also taken hold of many refugees fleeing their paradise behind the Iron Curtain. No (exile) publishers showed any interest in a text with this scope and content; this attempt to tell it as it is – where truth and lies, life and death, white and black are terms that cannot be compromised. An erosion of indifference and fear eats away at the river's bank, and civilization itself slowly but surely wastes away.

Those granted old age (born somewhere around 1910) have witnessed plenty of reversals in their lives. They've even lived to see the unthinkable: in the early 1990s Azerbaijani president Abulfaz Elchibey asked the United States and Russia to intervene with their respective militaries in his country's conflict with Armenia. At the time this book was written (i.e. 1975), something like this (which is only one of many "trivial" examples) could only have happened within the realm of absurdist literature. Today, not only communism but also socialism of the old era, that popular movement at one time dominating Western Europe's political scene, is irretrievably buried.

One of the bloodiest and most brutal period humankind ever went through, spanning the period of nearly a century, recently came to an end with the revolutionary events of 1989. This horrible period of totalitarian oppression was the work of criminals, whose crime – mass murders and the spiritual deadening of millions – has exceeded the statute of limitations and, consequently, remains unpunished. This does not mean that they were pardoned. Their crimes are ineffaceably etched into the hearts and thoughts of its countless victims.

But there's no need to erect gallows. A nation liberated from Bolshevik bondage is punishment enough. Their death sentence has to live in the country in which they once had absolute power. No one and nothing will ever replace their lost power.

But we must never allow them to forget. The useless lookout for what tomorrow brings and each word that reminds them of their former dominion over man is the present noose tightening around their necks and the nail driven, with each passing day of impotence, into their coffins. A spirit of freedom currently prevails; this is the greatest punishment.

JK

Barry's Bay, Canada, July 1997

I. *Defining the Essential*

And so it came to be one hundred and twenty-seven years ago. In the "Bildungsgesellschaft für Arbeiter" office in the English town of Bishopsgate, Liverpool Street 46, Marx & Engels' instructions on how to turn the world upside down first saw the light of day: The Communist Manifesto (1848). And it really did, in years to follow, turn the world as we knew it upside down. The opression of half of humanity behind the political system's barbed wire made person's unique and unrepeatable life meaningless. The spiteful class struggle between the small hierarchy of new-age rulers and the masses of the subjugated population will forever remain a horrid memento to the 20th century. The song of Marx & Engels' proletariat is the saddest of them all. It tells of a bird that gets just enough to eat to stave off starvation. Its wings lie motionless on the executioner's block. This is how the principles of the new political organization were laid out – in the south or west, north or east, all over the world, twenty-four hours a day, three hundred and sixty-five days a year and for decades on end it clung to one goal: to disrupt an individual's life by way of terror and constant subversive activities until it became unbearable – to break him in his spirit and his body. This activity, geared toward devastating a person's mental, moral and physical stability, is conducted by a relatively small group of terrorists: THE INTERNATIONAL COMMUNIST (terrorist and subversive) ORGANIZATION, abbreviated as IC(ts)O.

In our eyes, the holders of IC(ts)O cards are outcasts not belonging to any nation. They have no interest in solving or resolving civilization's current problems. The foremost goal of their activities is a longing for power over the miserable, humiliated and decent human being anywhere on earth. Obtaining this monstrous personal power, no matter if it's a little or a lot, automatically appeases the lust of sadistic tyranny; it is the driving power propelling this power-hungry group irrepressibly forward. As soon as the IC(ts)O members get this power – the proof of their absolute potency – they bond together out of fear that they will lose it.

As a result of this abnormal condition, the heartless shaking of humanity has acquired dimensions difficult to bear. As with a tree, the roots of a human soul undergo, day in and day out, a mismatched struggle with devastating tempests. Sooner or later, the exhausted slave falls to the ground, his joints crack and blood spills from him. Trampled ideas or those never expressed roll out of his broken head. Marx & Engels' vision of a new world order is carried out to the final detail. The killers of the 20th century, united in single file under the banner of the International Communist (terrorist and subversive) Organization, treat our unique and unrepeatable lives with the disregard of new-age slaveholders.

Destructive evil is the impetus for violence, and is permanently nestled in the soul of each person. Constructive good, destructive evil and the mutual relationship of these two antithetic powers systematically influence the spiritual condition and conduct of a human being. A person as such is never satisfied with himself or with the situation he presently finds himself in. The destructive evil of a dissatisfied human being usually emerges, provoked by inactivity, through the magnifying glass of self-analysis. He who thinks the IC(ts)O member never engages in self-contemplation is naive. The opposite is true. Self-critical thinking releases an inexhaustible amount of energy from a morally disturbed individual. All self-contemplation in the mirror reveals to a parasitic tyrant his own wretchedness. His disdain for himself is always vented in a self-degradation that is only expiable through an intoxicating victory over one's defenseless fellow-citizen. In the mirror of self-analysis, the bearer of the IC(ts)O card cannot escape his own blemishes. Lop ears, short legs, curved back or harelip are common. But most of the IC(ts)O members are not physically disfigured. They are only spiritually crippled. The moment the destructive evil in the soul of a person gains an edge over the constructive good, the loss of human decency always ensues. And just as birds of a feather flock together, people without decency associate with their own kind, with individuals afflicted with the same incurable illness – inferiority.

In its internal structure, the International Communism (terrorist and subversive) Organization rises to a point like a pyramid assembled from inferior compatriots, who have sold out to the idea of unchallenged personal power. The pyramid structure consists of the least satisfied, least capable and predominantly of the most primitive members of society.

1	X
2	XX
3	XXX
4	XXXX
5	XXXXX
6	XXXXXX
7	XXXXXXX
8	XXXXXXXX
9	XXXXXXXXX
10	XXXXXXXXXX

Half-man, half-beast, the zealous promoter of barbarism gains through membership to the pyramid a small, medium or large amount of (always monstrous) personal power. The corrosive feeling is then alleviated by bullying or by humiliating fellow citizens. This horde of dangerous primitives has never created and will never create anything beneficial or of value, but instead vehemently harasses, demolishes and erodes from the base, it falsifies and retouches as it pleases what is already finished, and above all devoutly serves its superiors and requires a slavish obedience from its inferiors.

The tenacious struggle to obtain a more powerful position over fellow citizens down in the streets has its beginnings, its firmly embedded roots, within the pyramid itself. The path upward or the irreversible fall depends on the ambitions and skin thickness of everyone, even the most self-important member of the ruling hierarchy. The more ruthless the jockeying for position within the lower layers, down in the murky waters of this ekaborated construction, the more ruthless the struggles among the ruling elite. The throne at the top of the anti-human pyramid is very rarely vacant, and only the most proficient of schemers utilizing all of his tricks of the trade has a chance to obtain the position of absolute ruler over the life and death of his subjects.

The concept of truth, the real essence of events and things, has in this day and age acquired for many an absurd meaning. In contrast, the thousands of small and great lies, the countless number of small and large murders, chameleonic words, treacherous theories on war and peace, friendship between nations, demagogical phrases and theories turned upside down on who man is, what he wants, what he needs and in which direction he must march to fulfill all his dreams, are fed to the half of humanity behind the barbed wire day in and day out for them to ruminate on like a cow on its cud with the rationalization that it's a scientifically based total truth, next to which any other alternative is an aberrant naivety. The exhausted citizen, forever someone's servant, dragged down a dusty trail to paradise by a pair of bulls, often gives in to the conditions of this dirty game. The dream of the truth, and of getting to the true essence of events and things, is then tucked away in the farthest corner of his soul and, for the time being and a long time to come, he bids farewell to it.

But for whatever reason, man never bids farewell for good to the dream of the truth and of getting to the true essence of events and things. His quenchless thirst for truth and justice always outlasts all horrors and lives through the generations even though many are persecuted for centuries. A truthful world is a world where the sun shines, the stars spread out in the night and birds fly through the sky. A happy human existence is not conceivable in an untruthful world. This kind of world turns with the help of artificially constructed theories; the sun does not shine there, the stars at night are covered by a curtain of darkness and the birds fall headlong like rocks to the earth. An individual, bound by the straitjacket of artificially constructed political theories, ceases to be a free person. Artificially constructed political theories, whose sole aim is to bind a person to submission, essentially contradict the truth, the real essence of historically substantiated events, things and human nature, and serve only to allow dictators of tyranny to grasp and maintain power.

Man can bend his back for a decade or even a century, but he won't bend it forever. As soon as the children of his children, or the children of their children see the light of hope, they will discover, with a candle in their hands, that kernel of truth tucked away in grandmother's cobweb-strewn chest, standing proud like a beautiful but crooked tree that has weathered a devastating storm.

The tragedy of life for every individual is that it is unrepeatable. A human being wants to live his unique and unrepeatable life in happiness from birth to final breath. Each human being is well aware that if he does not experience at least a little happiness during this unique period, his life is useless and wasted. The International Communist (terrorist and subversive) Organization makes full use of humanity's search and groping for happiness for its own benefit. This arises from the knowledge that generation after generation of the human population is divided into two parts of unequal size: the happiness-seeking majority, indefatigably wandering from town to town, from village to village, from the tip of the ploughed field to the one on the distant horizon, along paths and off paths. Then there is the power-seeking minority which boldly professes it knows the way to happiness; that it knows for certain beyond which hill, which cliff, which forest and valley happiness can be found. Thus it came to be that from the first day of the IC(ts)0's conception, armed with the artificially constructed political theory of The Communist Manifesto (1848), it assumed the role of the unabashed ruler over the happiness-seeking majority. But this leading role was never entrusted to the criminal minority by this majority of happiness-seeking people. The criminal minority took hold of the leading role by way of deceit, terror and subversive activities. For decades it has ruled the majority with an iron fist and never allowed the majority to discuss the shameless leading role of the minority, or to change anything about this abnormal state through a vote. The leading role of the communist minority everywhere the IC(ts)O minority is in power is a role fabricated and artificially constructed from the base: The communist minority has never and will never be about showing decent people the road to happiness.

This kind of deceitful minority that professes to know something, but only acts in its own power interests, is an evil minority. The deceitful machine of the evil minority, which has been running on full throttle to carry out its perfidious goals, can only be stopped at the cost of another world catastrophe. The criminal, who has firmly decided to achieve his criminal aim, will never voluntarily step aside. The roots of the criminal are roots of evil. The International Communist (terrorist and subversive) Organization is completely submerged in evil, and the spreading of evil is its primary mission. It's no wonder that two classes stand in opposition to one another in countries where IC(ts)O minority groups are in power: the ruling class and the class that is ruled; the class of communist predators and the people being preyed upon. This kind of state, of country, is then a state and country of mutual hatred. An irreconcilable, unending struggle exists between these two classes. The ruling class has the arms, the secret police, countless informers, the army, an extensive network of concentration camps and prisons, impermeable borders and all means of propaganda. The class being preyed upon has only its bare hands and beating hearts. The preyed-upon citizen is pressed into a dark corner with the threat that the dagger held before his eyes by the laughing tyrant will be mercilessly thrust through his beating heart if he does not lick in humiliation the shining blade. He is thus given the choice to decide between life and death. Assuming that this citizen is a worker in a nationalized factory for knives and daggers, the blade he is offered to lick is that of the dagger he himself produced.

The IC(ts)O utilizes to achieve its goals the destructive evil within each person – the darkest and most instinctive sides of the individual, worn out and exhausted by the surrounding evil. These characteristics, which, together with the good in a human being, comprise a perpetual struggle, are characteristics ineffaceably etched in his genes, and are passed on from one generation to the next as an integral part of an individual's personality. The fact that a person has two faces will remain now and forever a most indisputable fact – a decent face and a perverse one. The perverse side of each person is the sensitive chord on which IC(ts)O members play to seduce other willing and power-hungry followers to join. An organization based on the perverse characteristics of its members, and in which the performance of good is considered to be an emasculation undignified of man, is itself perverse.

People live in lands of natural beauty where they were born and call this land the fatherland, native land, homeland, country, beloved birthplace or home. Each home has its meadow, covered with a beautiful carpet of flowers, where the stalks of grass bend delicately to each other. One tree grows beside another, giving rise to a forest. Springs run off steep cliffs in sparkling waterfalls, streams run into brooks and brooks into violently rushing rivers. People live on this beautiful land. Each day they must do something so as not to die of hunger, to sustain themselves and their families.

The life-critical and existentially uncertain situation of each individual inhabiting this planet is the very life-critical and existentially uncertain situation which the IC(ts)O members, insidiously lurking in the shadows, await with open but treacherous arms. Man's constant pursuit of a livelihood is the substrate in the petrie dish. As night ends with the break of day, and the day is replaced with another night, hopelessness sets in, and fear of the future slowly but surely spreads. The first and foremost mission of the International Communist (terrorist and subversive) Organization is, on the one hand, to manipulate the beaten-down masses so that they have time for nothing other than self-preservation. On the other hand, they carefully sift through and lure into their web those who show the most ambition, in order to ensure that this humiliating deprivation continues.

The more exhausting the deprivation and the hungrier the individual they manage to catch in their trap, the more worried the mother or father. But the more shameless and ragged the slacker, to whom the tuxedo is worth more than noble human traits, the more dangerous and bloodthirsty the criminal, the duffer filled with envy, the incompetent braggart, informer, graduate of the university of terrorism in Moscow, the thief, murderer, prostitute, alcoholic, masochistic don, undertaker of his own unsuspecting parents, half-witted monster, paranoid flunky, untalented page fillers charmed by the social-realist novel, tool-less carpenters, canvas-less painters, unqualified doctors, Judases and gadabouts, the greater the guarantee they will faithfully and willingly serve the human anthill.

While each real working person is in his own way a creator and an artist, the IC(ts)O member neither works nor creates, but makes a living exclusively through political conniving. The pyramid member is thus neither creator nor artist, but an outgrowth of hatred. So, like a cow born with two heads, six legs and without lungs or a brain, the bureaucrat of the communist machine is born without basic human qualities needed to live fruitfully and creatively. And since he cannot live fruitfully and creatively, he focuses all his energies on gaining power over those who can. The communist is a parasite on the honest, creative and artistic work of others: a malformed abnormity that abreacts its physical and mental defects through its wicked activities. A wild herd of physically, and especially mentally impaired members of the IC(ts)O, who do not at all miss even the slightest sign of a fertile and creative life not corresponding to the norms and ideas of how the world around them should appear.

For the free world, the International Communist (terrorist and subversive) Organization is its archenemy – only one will be proclaimed the victor and the other the defeated in the inevitable struggle over life and death.

II. The Pied Piper's Children

My Friends! You'll recognize me by this pipe.
Don't ever hesitate to revolt! Don't hang your head.
The butterfly taps on the window with velvet wings.
Get ready – I'll soon play my song.
Follow me without fear!
You'll once again become a princess.
And you deserve to be a prince.

Paintings made hundreds of years ago hang in museums and galleries and on the walls of people's homes. On town squares and in courtyards and parks, sculptures, whose beauty makes us light-headed, slumber through an age-old dream. Since time immemorial, man has leafed through the pages of books merely to discover that, as with the paintings and sculptures, each page is a search for an answer to the eternal question: Who am I, where do I come from and where am I headed? But what if one day, despite all our efforts to protect everything dear and essential to us, we find the books in smoldering piles, the statues smashed into pieces and the paintings ripped out of their frames by ruthless demons? Who then amongst the desolate ruins will answer our questions? Where should we go? What should we do? Whom should we turn to? Whom should we believe? What then?

Then man lifts his head and listens intently. What if a miraculously uplifting voice is heard between heaven and earth? The blue-green ocean sparkles amiably, but from afar it is so boundless that there is nothing left to do but to hang his head again. The echoes from our cries blast through the cliffs like a gun salute, but the mountains on the horizon aren't even visible on the clearest of days. And then all at once – what's that we hear? Nothing wards off the sorrow of a defenseless person like a liberating song. Once again we realize how much music means to us in these trying times. Where would we be without the flute's music? Without the liberating melody of the Pied Piper? Velvety tones beckon the young and old to desert the land where pictures have disappeared from the walls of people's homes, where statues have vanished from parks and the ashes of book pages flitter in the air. There's no other choice in these dreary ruins but to hold one's tongue and cry.

Not a day or night passes without the refugee retracing his path over the mountain peaks, across the river and through the deep forest, away from the hopelessness in musical steps. Even after all these years, he recalls how his spirit was lifted on that long and arduous trail by the Pied Piper's tall presence: the feather in his cap, pointy nose, harlequin suit, spiral-toed shoes and thin fingers tirelessly gliding over his magical flute. One day runs into the next and, just as he did, other groups and individuals attempt to escape the land of tyranny to the land where there's still freedom. Yet despite all their efforts and despite the Pied Piper's helping hand, for the majority of citizens the excruciating dream of escaping from the communist stronghold remains an excruciating dream - a cruel trap of submission for the ensnared mortal.

Children will often accept four bare prison walls as their own, so long as their parents promise them that sooner or later they will return to their favorite toys. But how can they be made to understand that the devil has disguised itself as an angel and pretends to be filled with good intentions, settling in their homes forever?

The Pied Piper's children – the emigrants – whisper night after night into the dark: "What good is a pearl-laced jug, void of a single drop of water, to someone dying of thirst?"

The most ill-fated discovery of the 20th century, which has already driven so many from their homes and transformed them into emigrants, is indisputably the Marx & Lenin ideological-liquidation machine. The sole purpose of this monstrous machine, serviced and kept running by the International Communist (terrorist and subversion) Organization, is to ceaselessly turn noble and proud human beings into a humiliated, broken and self-flagellating obedient mass. Sooner or later the citizens become cogs - they resignedly fit together and click. They fall asleep with the hope that maybe tomorrow they'll wake from the nightmare.

In such a country where the terrorists and subversives, the IC(ts)O members have established their uncontrollable power, the communist-tyrant does not have the least bit of interest in the worker obtaining job satisfaction and earning a well-deserved rest with his happy family, in the scientist and philosopher working together on new theories that would ensure an acceptable future for humanity, in the musician composing what he hears, in the painter painting what he sees, in the writer writing what he thinks, in the sculptor chipping away at rocks with his hammer and chisel in harmony with his ideas: in other words, in people living proudly, greatly and open-mindedly as they are destined to do from their birth. The tyrant's only interest is the citizen's absolute obedience as part of his nationalized life. Among the gray buildings, on the gray streets, over the gray servile heads the banners proclaim only one thing: "Any sheep leaving the herd will feel the wrath of the old wolves' fangs."

The Marx & Lenin liquidation machine, whose old wolves' fangs are only one of numerous means to compel citizen obedience, has quite easy work. It runs as a self-lubricating unit. New-age perpetual motion. After his exertions from dawn to dusk, the exhausted citizen returns to his family, depressed by the never-ending glut of joyless news. The frustrated workers perform their jobs half-heartedly from payday to payday. Meanwhile the timorous philosophers analyze letter by letter each sentence supposedly written by Lenin. Composers celebrate any old Stalin fart with grandiose cantatas. Sculptors frantically cast busts of so-called proletarian presidents from pure gold Painters have their hands full working on the portrait of comrade John Doe, who appears to have the whole world lying at his feet. A bleak fate awaits those who refuse to lick the tyrants' paws. It doesn't take long for the henchmen to come calling at the door of such a desperado. The defenseless victim is, under the veil of the night, dragged out to the stubble fields where a vicious north wind blows. Soon the hungry wolves finish off with their fangs what the horrid Marx & Lenin machines began on the impoverished body and soul.

Many witnessing this from afar, beyond the protective bulwark of the iron curtain, cannot understand how an essentially prudent and ponderous people could, in the latter half of the 20th century, allow themselves to be made into mere cogs in such a monstrous machine; how they could let themselves be manipulated like despised slaves. They feel it's a waste of time to mention that a similar fate could someday happen to them. They ask why the cogs in the smothering Marx & Lenin machine have not long since stopped serving the machine; why they haven't revolted en masse; why they have not all left to hide away. Why the hideous machine didn't start rusting at the joints a half-century ago and why the creature hasn't fallen into a heap of scrap metal.

It's extremely difficult, perhaps even impossible, to explain to someone who's never experienced it what it means for a foreign army to enter the sacred ground of one's native country in the name of fraternal assistance and eternal friendship, and for this army to demand a sweeping embrace and adoring kiss for its apparent magnanimity and Slavic camaraderie. How could anyone who's never seen his own parents kneeling in humiliation in a muddy driveway, pleading for mercy or, if it came to that, willingly collaborating with the enemy, possibly begin to understand? Those asking themselves how an otherwise capable people could so easily become mere cogs in the machine still haven't had to cut free from lampposts the bodies of tortured brothers, sisters, friends or acquaintances. The talented violinist has never had to sink to the level of a worn-out fiddler in order to appease a murderer's ears from morning to night. The teary-eyed worker still hasn't had to bury a fellow colleague shot by the workers' militia. The doctor still hasn't been ordered to cease treating a patient, whose life this barbaric system doesn't have the least bit of interest in. The free person still hasn't had to live in a system so monstrous that in village after village, place after place and house after house an informer is watching, ready to report on the breath of each and every citizen he personally takes exception to, and to submit this detailed report to his or her high-ranking superior.

Sceptical and incredulous people of the free world! You've never had to live in a stronghold of treacherous rats, whose gluttony and uselessness, inferiority and blunt caginess, as well as their current unbelievable ability to destroy any part of your unique and thus unrepeatable life, is nothing more than a prototype of an enslaved society, in which two irreconcilable sides – you and the power-hungry barbarians – will battle to the last drop of blood.

Migrating birds fleeing winter for warmer lands instinctively assume that they'll be returning to their abandoned nests in the spring. A human being, leaving his native country because it is no longer possible to live there without feeling ashamed and powerless, is consoled by the thoughts that he'll someday be reunited with everything that was difficult to leave behind. In contrast to the happy swallow, however, spring rarely comes to the Pied Piper emigrants, and so the homecoming never takes place.

So much has changed over the past seven years! New pictures hang on the walls of new homes. New books fill the shelves of new bookcases. The nearby Statue of Liberty holds aloft her inextinguishable torch. Reports seep out from the abandoned home that rats, once completely grey, have turned red. And that's not all. Whereas long ago the cowardly aldermen begged the Pied Piper to get rid of all omnivorous rodents, the current rulers have promised the rats eternal friendship in return for the Pied Piper's head.

For the most part, the Marx & Lenin liquidation machine runs smoothly and faultlessly. The gears click and fall into place. At times, those tending the machine jump about with an oilcan to take care of any unpleasant squeaks.

III. The Soviet Union – The Promised Land

Such emptiness abounds, such vast suffocating sadness that can't even be viewed through a giant telescope on the surface of a dead planet, where nothing grows, there's no vegetation, nothing lives, neither bug nor plant, neither bird nor butterfly and there's no water or sun or air. Not even in the Sahara desert, in the most scorched and abandoned corner of Africa where only the vultures greedily tear rotting meat from the corpse of a stray zebra, can one be overcome with such a feeling of absolute helplessness. A lone castaway on a raft in the middle of the Pacific Ocean, after two hundred and forty-six days of solitude, half delirious from the effects of the ultraviolet rays and salt water would not die with a more profound sense of hopelessness.

Nothing can compare with life in this country: utter dilapidation, a fallen tree, the green isn't green, the blue isn't blue. Wherever the eye looks it sees ruins, splashed with an old coat of paint and tattered by mice, for which all cats have long since lost their appetite. All around you is gray – gray walls, gray buildings, gray skies in gray eyes, gray cars; even Moscow's Red Square is gray, gray Generalissimo, the gray university on Lenin Hill, gray tanks and gray missiles aimed at countries near and far where the unsuspecting poet pens his verses, the worker freely decides the course of his life, humble people hold discussions. There, in a blossoming park, happy children play, swinging on their swings until the gray scatterings of an explosion kills them all.

It's hard to say where people inhabiting this gray sixth of the world find the courage to show their faces to their fellowman. We know all too well that they don't have an ounce of shame in their bodies, but this doesn't mean that the cynic doesn't bear any responsibility for the crimes he's committed. Even though most of them crawl around degradedly on all fours in the mud of their gray life, without laughter or tears, it seems as if they're being formed by this very humiliation – poverty, mange and pox – into a mass of shameless and treacherous provocateurs. Humiliated citizens flock together in faceless masses during the day and in the evening, at night and at dawn, so as to mutually ensure that they get the most out of treachery, and that sooner or later their partnership in the monstrous system will yield the desired results. The faceless masses of the Russian Socialist Federated Soviet Republic, the Ukrainian Soviet Socialist Republic, the

Byelorussian Soviet Socialist Republic, the Uzbekistan Soviet Socialist Republic, the Kazakstan Soviet Socialist Republic, the Georgian Soviet Socialist Republic, the Azerbaijan Soviet Socialist Republic, The Lithuanian Soviet Socialist Republic, the Moldavian Soviet Socialist Republic, the Latvian Soviet Socialist Republic, the Kirghiz Soviet Socialist Republic, the Tajikistan Soviet Socialist Republic, the Armenian Soviet Socialist Republic, the Turkmenistan Soviet Socialist Republic and the Estonian Soviet Socialist Republic – blankly view the hazy future. Before them lies the vast, immense Soviet Union, the fruit of the Great October Socialist Revolution (1917), and they are its infamous descendants. It was never the intention of the revolution to build a civilized state cooperating with other willing states, but to transform the rest of the world into a similarly malformed society.

Nowhere else in the world is there a country that can boast of having such a high concentration of degenerating and senile ruling bureaucrats. These communist terrorist-subversives, sunk deeply into the armchairs of their positions of power within the pyramidal hierarchy, are kept alive by transplants for their rotting organs, by massaging their sclerotic hearts, and by oxidizing their collapsed lungs. They're given dentures, blood transfusions and rejuvenation injections, yet they leave nothing behind but an environmentally, economically and mentally destroyed country. In this kind of appalling place, the communist dictator becomes an obvious part of a person's birth and death, waking and sleeping. The citizen no longer cares that he can never leave the mindless herd and live something other than a nationalized life. A happy individual is salt in the eyes of the organizers of collective life. Language, the unique and natural form of a people's mutual understanding (to speak as one naturally learns), is deformed by the elite of the pyramidal bureaucracy through its constant rehashing of vulgar slogans in the guttural shrieks of a cowardly nation. A measly document, Marx & Engels' instructions on how to recreate the world so that it nauseates everyone, found its most fertile soil in a former czarist empire. A sixth of the world's inhabitants, willing propagators of these assorted ideas, painstakingly deformed themselves into a submissive and obedient herd of disturbed wretches. But we cannot shed tears for these disturbed wretches who tore their own tongues from their mouths and are even trying to yank them from the mouths of those who are not afraid to speak the truth.

The Great German Empire (Deutschland, Deutschland, über alles) was enveloped by thick smoke from the smoldering ruins of a destroyed fascism. Berlin served out its term as the Fuhrer's headquarters. The sparks of expansive communism leapt forth from the Soviet Union in all directions. The Generalissimo named

Moscow the new centre for worldwide thuggery. On the very day that Adolf Hitler and Eva Braun committed suicide, Stalin's thugs picked up the smoldering torch of fascism and set out on the path well worn by their former opponent. Just as two gangs of thugs specializing in murdering peaceful inhabitants cannot exist side by side on the same street, neither can two states, one fascist and the other communist, whose common underlying principle is that of terror and a world buckled to its knees, exist side by side under a single blue sky in the international tiltyard. These two gangster states will then engage in a ruthless life-or-death struggle until one of them is destroyed.

Fascism was destroyed by the rise of communism, and the International Communist (terrorist and subversive) Organization seized power over all territories inhabited by exhausted and tyrannized people during World War II. The callous gangster ended up victor in the fight over the number of square kilometers, natural resources and production potential (i.e. the spoils of war) of the population. The transfer of power from the hands of one thug to those of another thug brought no relief to the peaceful parts of the world. It was soon evident that the ideology, plans and goals of the victorious gang of thugs were identical to those of the defeated gang. The definition of the ideology, plans and goals of the International FASCIST (terrorist and subversive) Organization is currently the definition of the ideology, plans and goals of the International COMMUNIST (terrorist and subversive) Organization. In other words, fascism is dead. The unfortunate outcasts pursued by boundless terror rightly call out: "Death to communism!"

One cannot overlook the obvious fact that World War III has not broken out over the past 30 years, despite conditions being ripe for it on numerous occasions. In contrast to Hitler's thundering weapons, the IC(ts)O is gradually working toward its final goal to rule the world – step by step with a patient and stealthy deceptiveness. It sets people's homes on fire in cold blood only to watch from a distance with anonymous civility to see if the inhabitants manage to extinguish the spreading flames. Peaceful cooperation with the democratic part of the world afraid of vigorously intervening against the deceitful arsonist in the name of democracy, democratic freedom and principles has only helped the new-age aggressors win the undeclared war and thus subjugate millions of other lives. The sower's calculating hand plants the seed of unrest in the hope that evil will sooner or later prevail over good. His guiding principle is that the seed of dissatisfaction blossoms in the fertile soil of mutual hatred among people, and that ripe fruit in the form of an undermined and disorganized world will fall effortlessly into his hands.

If, on the one hand, we can call Moscow and the USSR a

darkened cave where the arsonist dwells and prepares his future sinister plans, the same city and country is the dwelling place for the tombs of a generation whose views have dug a deep hole in which it is dying an undignified death, buried alive. This generation, born in 1917 as shots were fired from the battleship Aurora anchored in a St. Petersburg port, is now in 1975, fifty-eight years old. Born in terror and accompanied and raised by terror their whole lives, they are dying as miserably as they were born.

Fault lies in the failures of the Soviet Union's population to recognize the terror early on, the intentional lack of action in protesting gross violations of basic human rights, the disinterest in firmly standing up face to face to despotism and snipping it in the bud from which the accountable part of this despotic system grew. Most of the inhabitants actively or passively support the communist-terrorist government: Over the past fifty-eight years there has yet to be the faintest hint that they wish to change anything. With their resounding YES the people of the Union of Soviet Socialist Republics rank among the most shameless and malicious creatures capable of anything. In assuming an affirmative position toward tyranny, they are laying the foundation for the creation of an offshoot of a species unprecedented in the history of anthropology: the communist person – *Homo barbaricus*.

The central world communist pyramid in Moscow
with subservient sub-pyramids

If, in fact, the shameless fascist creatures inhabiting Germany were creatures fanatically infatuated for a short period with the Fuhrer's seductive image of racial supremacy and their predetermined fate to rule the world, the shameless communist person – Homo barbaricus – inhabiting the USSR is not a fanatical creature, but a devoted servant to a fascist ideology in communist form. The fascist ideology has only one goal in its communist practice: to quickly solidify its absolute power by liquidating any inconvenient opposition, and with the help of collaborating governments to take control of territories of countries not yet servile to the communist cause and, if they can, over as much of the world as possible – and after surrounding America and finally destroying it, to rule the entire world.

By gradually carrying out this plan which it has advanced through the sub-pyramidal center of absolute power, by identifying its absolute world power with the sense of everyday events, the shameless creatures of the USSR give their absolute consent to having their lives begun, run and ended in this nationalized way. The road through a nationalized life is a cold-blooded glare into the eyes of hundreds, thousands and millions of cold corpses which have paved the way. The shameless creatures of the USSR leave in their wake piles of burnt books, hacked apart paintings, crucifixes torn down and replaced by the crucified proletariat, thinkers disposed of through hallucinogenic injections, maimed musical virtuosos or simple farmers, stripped of the possibility of reaping what they have sown. A day doesn't pass by in which dozens of inhuman resolutions are submitted for the willing soviet masses to sign at nationalized workplaces. Each signature means the torturing of more than one inconvenient fellow citizen and the suffering of entire nations, populations of other countries held by the reigns of submission in the hands of collaborating governments. The map of the world looks like the bristly body of a spider, viciously spanning the globe from pole to pole.

The free world marches forth down a difficult road and free people live a brave, independent and creative life. We call this kind of road the one less traveled, one filled with discoveries. All hardships and mistakes are then the hardships and mistakes of new discoveries and of the acts of a brave, independent and creative person. The road of the Union of Soviet Socialist Republics is an old and well-worn road of terror, sly tricks, military intimidation, occupation and the breaking of stubborn spines. This road is then the road of imitating, copying and adopting all violence of the past. The mistakes and hardships are mistakes and hardships of the executioner, who has to shoot three times before hitting the innocent victim. He who shamelessly declares to the entire world that imitating, copying, adopting and glossing over all cruelties of the past makes the Soviet Union something the whole world should marvel at is indeed treacherous, mendacious and ridiculous. The fact that those still free do not marvel at it but, instead, quake in fear that they are not inflicted with a similar misfortune and that those already swamped by it fear being completely submerged, serves only to increase the rage of the International Communist (terrorist and subversive) Organization and to raise its level of terror.

Soviet communism has exceeded German fascism both horizontally and vertically – in both depth and width. Feigning unawareness or ignorance, confusion or crazed blindness in today's world of obvious lies and obvious truth, obvious evil and obvious good does not rinse the responsibility for crimes committed by the hands of the creators and co-creators of these deformations. Fifty-eight years have passed since 1917, and after such a long period of time it has to be apparent to each and every individual comprising the submissive and mindless masses in the land of the so-called first socialist state that the road taken by the Great October Socialist Revolution is a road of sweeping violence and uncontrollable evil. As soon as the citizen allows himself to become part of the mindless and all-willing masses, he falls into the communist dictator's trap, from which he can only escape through his own death. Whoever accepts his unenviable portion of deceitful porridge with a shrug of the shoulders, or whoever does not call the trap inhuman, participates in the creation and operation of this monstrous system. This is the only way that people become both prisoners and bloodthirsty jailers in a totalitarian state. Murderers and murder victims. Defilers and the defiled. Torturers and the tortured. Slaveholders and slaves.

For the first time over the past thousands of years of the existence of various forms of the tyranny of man by man, the one in shackles is not fighting or hoping for freedom; tears of distress for tomorrow do not run down his face; he does not tear his hair out in desperation over the dim future for his descendents; he doesn't think to change his life by assassinating the tyrants in his unenviable life; he doesn't escape from his vast ghetto through an underground tunnel; he doesn't scream himself hoarse over the suppressed truth and the right to justice; he doesn't shed tears over the fiery pages of a beloved book, but instead does all he can to ensure that those still free and proudly standing become part of his deformed system. Only by wiping out all differences between the prisoner and jailer, the murderer and victim, the defiler and defiled, the torturer and tortured, the slaveholder and the slave and between the tyrant and the tyrannized will the revolution commenced in Russia in 1917 be ceremoniously declared a final victory. The period from commencement to finality, from beginning to end, from the start of the slaughter to the piles of cold corpses, will enter into history as the period in which all differences between a human being and an animal were wiped away.

Normally, one would commiserate with a people subjugated and inflicted with misfortune, would offer them a helping hand and words of solace, or even fight for their freedom. But we wish, from the bottom of our hearts, that the spiteful and immoral citizens of the Union of Soviet Socialist Republics devour to the last crumb what they so eagerly cooked up for themselves.

IV. An Emigrant's Report on a Natural Catastrophe in the Snow-Covered Mountains Near His Hometown of Nejezchleby

A natural catastrophe struck in the snow-covered Carpathian Mountains, near my hometown of Nejezchleby. An avalanche broke loose in the valley beneath the highest peak, the Great Mushroom (912 meters), and buried me alive. I couldn't move an inch in that freezing cavity. Rescue workers were soon probing the deep snow with sticks. It didn't dawn on me who those rescuers could be. How had they arrived so quickly and why were they acting as if it didn't matter if they found me dead or alive? It seemed as if they were going to probe the snow just long enough to poke my body. Only then, after I was pinned down like a butterfly, would they be assured that I would never again escape from this country.

At that moment, the sun's ray broke through the several meters of stiffened snow and flooded my body. I was imprisoned in an embryonic position between the walls of the frozen slot. Against my hot breath the glossy snow soon acquired the characteristics of an ice mirror. I caught my reflection, my pale face awaiting death, right at the moment when one of the probing sticks penetrated my heart and brought it to a stop. With cynical thoroughness, the rescuers had pierced my heart in the avalanche not far from my hometown. They wanted to be sure that they'd finally stripped me of the chance to flee to freedom. After all, they hated nothing more than a butterfly, especially one with beautiful colors, which flies wherever it wants.

The funeral preparations were made the next day in the village of Nejezchleby, in the Upper Nádvořiště region, where I was born forty-two years before. Instead of my parents placing me piously in a coffin and covering the horrid spectacle with the coffin's lid, they sat me on the bench in the corner of an enormous kitchen between the stove and a cracked wall. I leaned to the side like one of those wax dolls in a house of horror. The fire crackled in the stove. The doors, slightly ajar, cast mysterious signs on the ceiling. My left hand, touching the hot stove, softened like butter, while the other, the right hand, pressed against the unheated wall, turned blue from the incessant cold.

The villagers trickled by, one after another, in an endless procession. Childhood friends from school and elsewhere bid emotional farewells, damp handkerchiefs clenched between their fingers. Curious passers-by or those who really didn't know me merely gave a nod. They'd seen it all before.

Sometimes I'd be left alone in the spacious kitchen. I'd use these moments to have a look around. A torch burned by the window. I couldn't understand why. The entire village had been connected to electric power long ago. A crucified Christ lay in a nook in the wall. His half-exposed stomach was covered with decomposing flies. They dropped there dead with exhaustion from spring to fall. A bowl of fruit balanced on the edge of a worn table. Over-satiated worms crawled out of yellowish apples into the rearly morning gray. A dried-up wreath of garlic hung from a ceiling beam. The first signs of dawn could be glimpsed through the window. In the distance, beyond the village's hilly fields, I could hear ice floes on the Orava River crashing into each other. My older sister Šárka swung on the garden swing. She held a white ball between her legs. I could see a smiling black woman pushing her. But the scene was chaotic, and I only had a partially realistic view of the things around me. The black woman was the one I had read about in Harriet Beecher Stowe's Uncle Tom's Cabin as a 13-year-old boy. The garden swing was held up by the wind. The vision of my sister with a white ball on her lap did not correspond to reality. I have no siblings.

A shuffling of boots, the hacks and whispers of curious villagers were heard through the door from the entry hall. As soon as they'd assembled a large enough group, they came in for another visit. Many of them came to see me two or three times. Now and then someone would kneel by me and gaze long and hard into my eyes that had yet to be pressed closed. Some of them stuck out their tongues or thumbed their noses at me. They tried out all the buffoonery they could on me. If they made me laugh, it was all the proof they needed that I was only putting them on.

Around half past four in the morning, one of the rescue workers drifted in from the mountains. He had apparently run the whole way. He was sweating so much he smelled like an overworked horse. Chunks of snow were rapidly melting in his matted hair. Water ran down his neck. He knelt before me and jeered like the other village clowns. But when I didn't so much as blink, he didn't think twice and punched me fiercely in my head which slammed into the stove with a thud.

My parents looked on through the slightly open doors without the least sign of protest. It even seemed as if – but perhaps I just imagined this – a hint of consent with the rescuers' acts could be read in their still, narrowed eyes. Together with the others, like a can full of sardines with the lid off, they gazed impassively into the kitchen, as if the rescue worker had merely pounded his fist into a sack of rotten potatoes for the fun of it.

There is no greater anguish for the emigrant than a bad dream about his return to the country he escaped from. As the years go by, such a nightmare is our damnation. A refugee, who mooned the tyrants and found a new home in a faraway land and then is caught in an avalanche near his hometown, feels like an animal surrounded from all sides by a forest fire. Freedom is lost again.

The saddest part of it all is seeing my own parents. They helplessly watch the funeral of their child in the way the state-established morals dictate. They shiver and press against each other like a timid pair of partridges in the high grass awaiting the hunter's shot. If the hunter's aim is off, the hound will go after its prey. They are paralyzed by fear at what is to be their final farewell to their son, guilty only of his desire for freedom. They are relieved to be informed that, due to unfavorable weather conditions, the body of their child – the traitor – will remain imprisoned in the folds of the avalanche until summer comes, if not forever. This information at least temporarily spares them from the consequences of public backbiting, from the icy looks of their fellow citizens, from interrogations regarding the fugitive's identity and even from participating in the funeral, which is at any rate just a hasty wiping away of the traces of this unfortunate event.

We then ask how some parents allowed their own lives to literally slip through their fingers to such an inglorious end. If we could pose this question to them in private, eye to eye, we would receive their answer after some agonizing moments. They wouldn't manage without some coughs, a few shrugs, slouching and waving their arms about. They would refer to dead presidents, international conferences and peace agreements that were never observed. They would draw on the first and second world wars and enumerate how many times those, in whom they adamantly believed, sold out. But, they would whisper in despair. "That's nothing in comparison with the horror we have to live through now." They would declare themselves absolutely helpless. Nevertheless, a few bold Mothers and Fathers let themselves be heard. They would interrupt with the suggestion that the assassination of the Nazi, Reinhard Heydrich in Prague in 1942 be repeated, and that some of the hated communist slaveholders be taken out as soon as possible. But who will be the first to take up arms? Who will give the signal to attack? Who's not afraid to lay his own life on the line? When will the nation finally rise up as one and wash the dirty shame from itself in a bloodbath?

From the day the International Communist (terrorist and subversive) Organization first seized power in Czechoslovakia, the longing to pay the tyrant back eye for eye and tooth for tooth has lingered in the minds of many citizens. Yet, as years of waiting and indecisive procrastination pass by, the people have not only lost their courage for brave deeds, but have also begun to fear one another. The lifelong friend suddenly begins to act like a treacherous coward. Everyone's favorite neighbor, who used to go up a floor every Thursday to play cards, now spies from his window and writes down the names of all those who go to play cards since he stopped playing. Parents don't trust their children, and children don't trust their parents. The frustrated son often informs on his father or the mother on the daughter just so that place in the sun, which they sold themselves out for, isn't changed by an errant step into an errant step off the money train, and 30 Judas silver coins under the pillow aren't turned into a pile of dry leaves.

The way in which a zealous rescue worker pinned me to the frozen bed in the snow-covered Carpathian Mountains, once again entrapping me in the avalanche, speaks for itself. The nightlong preparations for my final trip in the privacy of the kitchen and the deplorable behavior of the guests in mourning represent the defiled world, in which people behave shamelessly because of their fear of being accused of sympathizing with the traitor. It is in this kind of corrupt world that salespeople are not salespeople, laborers are not laborers, flax growers are not flax growers, taxi drivers are not taxi drivers, piano virtuosos are not piano virtuosos and parents are not parents but instead are small bits of grain crushed by the abrasive surfaces of millstones.

The prohibited desertion of communist territory is punished by one's heart being stopped by the stick of a rescue worker in an avalanche. Each step out of line is met with a shove from corner to corner; from one dark room to one still darker, to only the worst paid job or to a physically exhausting position. The noose progressively tightens around the neck of the suffocating subject and is loosened or taken off in direct correlation to the position taken on that day, hour or minute toward this deviant world. Except for disrupted sleep, a little food and a monitored toilet break, nothing is allowed without the prior approval of spies, rescue workers, coordinators, regulators, informers or supervisors. Their monotonous buzz of conversation follows a citizen's every movement from dawn to dusk.

Communist terror is like a chemical substance possessing the properties of a narcotic gas. Released in dosages from a putrid tank, it creeps low to the ground and sneaks through cracks into private homes. Tasteless, odorless, inhaled fully by the unaware father, mother and innocent children, it has a devastating effect on the human mind. Only the most prudent – those expecting danger – fill cracks and crevices with old rags hoping to survive. These few maintained their faith that someday the free world would return. In such a world salespeople will once again be willing to sell, laborers will devote themselves to honorable work, flax growers will grow flax, taxi drivers will drive taxis, piano virtuosos will dizzy their audiences with their virtuosity. Parents will no longer have to watch helplessly as Red Guards stop the ascent of their children toward the sun, causing an Icarian fall in mid-flight.

Around eight in the morning the overheated kitchen resembled a steam bath, making breathing difficult. As soon as the dissatisfied rescuer ran out, most likely back to the mountains for more prey, Arnošt appeared in the doorway. We used to go to school together, but then he disappeared from sight. When he returned to the village some time later, he boasted that he could speak fluent Russian. He didn't hold any public position, but everyone knew that if it came to it, he would be responsible for running the village smoothly. As darkness fell, he'd wander from house to house and listen under windows to what people were talking about. Quite a few times I caught him swinging on our garden swing. We would have preferred him to knock first and ask for permission.In contrast to the preceding clowns, Arnošt did not kneel before me. He didn't even pull any faces to make me laugh. Instead, he ostentatiously crossed his arms. He stood so close to me that our knees almost touched. He stank of brandy. Apparently, he'd needed to gain some courage before coming to see me.

The sun had lit up the sky outside, but was presently hidden behind the clouds. A pair of spotted geldings stood by the picket fence. Soon they would carry me away from here. The torch in the kitchen was now burning much more clearly; the flame had increased. So much so that it threatened to catch the dry wreath of garlic, and from there the entire house, but this immediate danger seemed to be the least of the worries of those present. Slandering denouncements began to percolate between Arnošt's teeth. He made sure that everyone in the hall understood him clearly. His first bone to pick was that I was even born. If I hadn't been born, I wouldn't need a funeral, he sarcastically declared. But that wasn't the real problem. In a maudlin voice he enumerated the pains and troubles a mother giving birth has to go through to honor her homeland. Through her extraordinary feat she breeds batches of highly conscientious workers – the future of the nation. As everyone knows, a highly conscientious comrade working tirelessly builds a much more promising tomorrow than the gloomy past. Not only did Arnošt know the exact year, month, day and hour of my birth, he even described the infamous occurrence with such vivacity and obvious disgust, that he himself might have assisted in the delivery room.

Arnošt described me to the sardines in the entry hall as a childhood bigmouth, a candy and a snack thief who stole from my needy classmates, and now a big-shot traveler who thinks he can come and go as he pleases: in short, as if there hadn't been a more demonic nitpicker in the long history of an otherwise orderly village. The people were most surprised to learn that my life had always been the life of a cursed horsefly, who, masked as a human, flew around the village for decades and inconspicuously bit cows to death, which were much more useful. When he pointed out that horseflies never buzz, but approach their victim in stealthy silence like an assassin on tiptoes, the guests in mourning began to wave their arms, as if I had just risen out of the stove and was circling overhead. The accusation of the basest crime came at the end: I had left my official place of residency without permission. "You!" said Arnošt, pointing his forefinger at me. "You, are even more repulsive than the fly on the corpse of the mourned revolutionary."

Soon the harnessed geldings carried me to a hayrack beneath a hill. Four of my sturdy uncles then hoisted me on their shoulders and carried me up into the woods. I wasn't even allowed to be buried among my ancestors. Whenever the pallbearers slipped in the mud, the coffin would lurch to one side. It was drizzling and the old coats, spread across the coffin in place of a proper cover, crackled in their wetness. I didn't weigh much, as if I'd been sitting by the stove for at least a week. Not even an animal will accept food in captivity. If I'd been seated and stretched out my hand, I could have touched my father or mother. We were that close. My uncles and parents were the only participants in the funeral procession. Once, when the trail was at its steepest, I could see down into the valley. Beneath the hill in a bluish haze I could make out the geldings' massive bodies. The smiling black woman held my older sister Šárka's hand. They passed the time feeding horses.

No one cried as my four uncles began to lower me into the deep hole. My mother gazed into the forest. Long ago we used to go there together to collect firewood. My father looked determinedly at something in the distance. When everything was ready, my uncles removed their hats, but if they were praying it wasn't heard in the redolent, late-winter fullness of my native land. Then someone came running up with the forgotten lid. A warm darkness enveloped me. As the frozen earth pelted the coffin, I never once forgot that it was only a bad dream. I remained calm and composed. In the worst moments, unless we allow our minds to be seized with absolute hopelessness, life does not end, but slowly regenerates. Then, using a cane, we stand, take two steps and feel better. Our legs will once again serve us, and our mind understands what it's doing.

V. Workers

Since the beginning of time man has used the most varied means to fight off death. The engineer speeds the train to escape his unenviable fate along the glowing rails in the foggy distance. The whistle's shrill warning gives all contemplating suicide time to reconsider. High in the mountains, under the castle ruins a bent old woman is trying to extract from the soil a magic herb for longevity. Meanwhile, a strange cocoon in a spacesuit walks on the surface of the moon, searching for signs of life. This no longer comes as a surprise to anyone. Yet we ask: "Did you find immortality there, friend?"

Man's undying attempts to preserve his sanity in a maddening world have been described in countless tales. These are tales about humanity pursuing freedom from death. The watchmaker deftly repairs the clock, but is never able to stop time. Renowned surgeons dissect each corpse with the unwavering hope that they will finally fish out an immortal soul. If not a soul, then at least some piece of evidence one exists. There isn't a mountain peak on the face of the planet that courageous mountaineers fear scurrying up. There isn't a volcano or deep abyss that ever-searching geologists aren't curious enough to inspect. There isn't an ocean wave that a ship avoids sailing through to reach the distant horizon. This tells us: "Only God knows why people plod onward knowing one's life must end!"

The worker defies death the most tenaciously of all. He labors all his life with bare hands. His muscles flex to the point of breaking. Many dig faithfully with their pickaxes in the rocky terrain from morning to night to earn enough for a dry hunk of bread. They could ask the bystanders: "Why aren't you the ones digging this hole?" The worker never asks these questions. He never calls his work humiliating or pointless. Shortly after his birth, three fairy godmothers gathered around his crib with their blessings. The first says: "I grant you wisdom." The second says: "You will weather all storms." The third declares: "When death finally comes, it will find you worthy."

By and large, death avoids struggling with the worker. When life's waning moments are upon him, death stands patiently aloof. It behaves with respect. Death finds it difficult to end the life of a good person. But when some leech or a dreaded murderer refuses to cooperate, the walls get splashed with blood. Whenever an honorable worker dies, the sheets remain as white as freshly fallen snow. The mordant laugh of the grim reaper with his scythe does not echo from the dark corners long into the night. Death doesn't propose a toast to his completed work with a concoction from the boiled bones of an old rogue. He doesn't consider it a victory to win out over the worker, just a formality. If truth be told, the reverence shown toward the worker by the absolute ruler over the lives of all earthly creatures is often the only and most precious reward for his lifelong toil.

An honest worker is born to be an honest worker. The telltale mark of this individual is his kindness and wisdom. The worker's wisdom is as unique as his means of livelihood. It's a wisdom gained from the school of life. The worker makes a living through the untiring use of his hands, his impassioned heart and by the habit of absorbing everything that encourages in a positive way the independence of his thinking. His talent comes from the ability to breathe life into lifeless matter. He uses his natural gifts to coordinate a thousand movements into one integral sequence in the creative process. He can hit a nail on its head blindfolded, make a hot brick from clay, quarry rocks into a marble fountain, a piece of smoldering iron into a horseshoe for the hoof of a wild horse, fashion gold into a dazzling cross high up on the church's vault, transform a forest into timber and timber into countless homes in which tired people live and rest.

Through his calling, the worker provides fellowman with a wide variety of necessities. Without even giving it a second thought, people use the worker's products day in and day out. Being a quiet and modest apprentice was passed down to the worker from his father, and to his father from his industrious father. A firm will to never stain the nobility of his humble origins runs through his body and mixes with his blood. The importance of feeling useful was instilled in the worker by his mother, who raised and taught him to appreciate this. There is no other way than to feel profound respect, just as for omnipotent death, for the life work of a human being who was born a noble worker and dies a noble worker. To preserve his dignity and to persevere in refusing enticing offers and becoming a turncoat, to not allow his body, soul, heart and independent thinking to be conned by the other side by a treacherous trick, and never betray himself and his sacred misson – this is the day-to-day struggle of the honest worker.

Nothing is more foreign to the honest worker than the beggar's tune some sing into the ears of communist henchmen when asking for favors. Not even an exorbitant sum of money can entice him to be dishonest. As soon as the worker accepts the golden egg as a reward for his dishonesty and then another bribe to betray his fellowman, the worker's unique role, his indispensable participation in turning the world into a better place ceases to exist. His precise share in the creation of a civilized society loses all meaning. His errant step is also his last step - he himself irrevocably disappears off the ledge of an abyss.

No other human is exposed to so much deception as a worker in a totalitarian state. The attempts to divert the worker from his predetermined path is the constant preoccupation of his communist rulers. They are members of a spineless and anti-human organization who have developed and put into practice a spineless and anti-human compilation of misleading theories - Marx & Engels' Communist Manifesto (1848) - with one goal in mind: to seize power over the worker. With ruthless calculation, new-age slaveholders have taken advantage of the fact that the worker longs for nothing more than to make a living with his own hands for himself and his family. They lure him, trying to get him to join their ranks using the biggest red lollipop on earth.

For the honest worker surrounded by the monstrous system of snares, decoys and boobytraps, who refuses to have anything to do with the alluring lollipop, life becomes hell on earth. As punishment, he has to sieve sand with his bare hands. He's only allowed to staunch the blood from his wounded hands once in a while with his own tongue. But no matter what happens to the honest worker, no matter what wrongs he must endure, he never leaves the battlefield defeated – he never sought to defeat anyone. The honest worker born to an honest worker does not long for power over his fellowman, nor does he dream of punching him, walking over him with muddy boots or sticking his head into a vat overflowing with human excrement.

The worker to whom honor is of the utmost importance walks down difficult paths in complicated circumstances. To navigate his way in accordance with his beliefs, he is guided by a set of commandments: he should never divert from the one and only mission he is destined to undertake; he should never commit a transgression by denouncing his place on earth; he must never, if only by his gullibility, attempt to lick the biggest red lollipop in the world; he must never do anything dishonest and never deny his inherited calling - but then, if he does, he will separate himself from his honorabale past and inevitably become a different person.

The turncoat's twisting path to the communist pyramid's upper levels is a path of ruthless disposal of all obstacles in the way and burning of crossed bridges. From morning to evening the initiates soak their hands in hot spa water to soften and whiten them as soon as possible. They then cover the remnants of calluses with gloves similar to those worn by fancy chauffeurs. In this act of betrayal, they not only separate themselves once and for all from true workers, but also become their most sadistic supervisors. The pure, inherited calling is hung out to dry in the wind for all to laugh at. These renegades have traded their principles and honesty for the pleasure and advantages of political power. The worker who sells his soul automatically becomes an ardent and loyal activist – one of the so-called working-class elite. Just as birds of the same feather flock together, clansmen of the working-class elite are for one another the dearest and most sought-after companions. What a sight this pack of communist carpetbaggers, half-wits, paroled jailbirds, liars, swindlers and good-for-nothings! What a sight this herd of deadbeats and traitors, for whom nothing is as repulsive as honest work, which most of them had always shirked.

The working-class elite is a group of international clansmen, who have cast aside their fathers, kicked aside their mothers and sold off their homeland. If we choose the thoroughbred horse as the proletariat symbol, then the members of the antihuman pyramid have abused this horse, swung themselves insidiously up into its saddle and, with a whip and spurs, flogged the poor creature to its certain death. In effect, the working-class elite are murderers of their mothers, the mothers of their children and the children themselves. The members of the IC(ts)O, whose core consists of the working-class elite, are enthroned on the top – they're new-age Herods, hustlers of human lives in the 20th century.

If the worker is allowed to carry on with his work under favorable conditions, then his satisfaction and self-confidence is solid security for all of us. In contrast, he who is prone to manipulation and then pits himself against someone or something is a robotic inciter symbolizing a candle with darkness beneath it. Forcing the womb of dissatisfaction on the working class and the twisted misuse of this intentionally provoked state to obtain their own selfish power interests represents the strategy, the battle plan, that a handful of two-faced schemers has managed to usher into the life of the communist movement. The advantageous pyramidal shape of the monolithic structure allows it to overlook the scope of the worker's dissatisfaction. From this pretentious throne, it regulates the masses in accordance with the designs of its long-term plans. No other political machinations, no other power-propagandistic superstructure, no other phantasmagoric lumpen-proletariat has managed to inflict so much harm on the working class as the International Communist (terrorist and subversive) Organization. The core of the pyramid is made up of the working-class elite. For them the honest worker is nothing more than a piece they move at will on a chessboard.

It's enough just to look up at the imponderable depths of the night sky. We find there in the vast constellations the eyes of millions of nameless labourers worn to death in state factories, on state battlefields, in concentration camps, mines, smelting houses, by constructing highways and dams, in state straitjackets in nationalized institutions for the insane. The things the worker has to suffer through and listen to from the owners of the big red lollipop before he dies! So many lies and deceits, the ideological and pseudo-philosophical distortions, the defamations, false smiles, insults, manifestos, empty promises, articles, laws and antihuman measures. So much fool's gold concealed by political phraseology that was to lead the working class to equality, mass security and the inalienable right to happiness. So many sacks with Judas silver have fallen on the spit-stained table in front of the worker's eyes. So many charming apparatchik-grooms have already offered engagement rings to working-class brides, even though by marriage they mean nothing more than deceitful polygamy. While honest workers are quietly dying, sucked into oblivion by tyranny, everything in this world is rosy red for the owners of the big red lollipop. Red banners and red busts of the maniacal revolutionaries, red power and the red throne of the kingdom. The International Communist (terrorist and subversive) Organization and the members of its core – the working-class elite – despise nothing so much as a shovel stuck before them into an overflowing pile of sand. Although they call themselves the vanguard of the working class and of the entire imperialist-oppressed proletariat, and they seize power and solidify it in the name of the worker, they shun him with disgust; nothing produces more of a foul smell for them, awakens more of a feeling of revulsion in them; they despise nothing more and flee from nothing with such horror as from the noble and honest worker and from working-class and proletarian labor. They despise the honest worker as they would a mangy dog and would never break bread with him. For the IC(tp)O member, the honest worker is a mangy dog that deserves nothing more than for its bent back to be whipped.

Communist hoodlums encircle the world, the most deceitful and merciless conquerors of working-class life to date – the slaveholders of the 20th century. They strangle everything living, everything beautiful, everything wise and everything with vitality – everything that stands in their way. They then let thistles grow in the bloody trail they leave behind. This weed is the fruit of their unbridled depravity.

VI. *The House on the Hill*

All human beings are born free and equal in dignity and rights.
(Eustafan)

In the search for an answer to a question a persecuted person would ask, or a family trying to escape the guardians of tyranny, or a musician whose music is forbidden in public, a painter whose painting is vandalized by secret police thugs, a writer whose book is in flames on top of a bonfire made of thousands of other books, a worker whose ingenious work is blacklisted as counter-revolutionary by his revolutionary masters, or the same question all emigrants would ask - for this purpose, to find an answer, I envisioned a place - A House on the Hill - where Eustafan lives.

He is a mythical figure, a prophet. His wisdom equals his personal experience. So when we ask him the one question which burdens us the most: "How is it possible that humans can inflict so much misery on other humans?", Eustafan says: "First give me your hand, then give me your heart and then give me your inner self. In return I give you the same. That is why humans are humans. They never inflict harm on others, they never betray a friend, they never lie to themselves or to anybody else. It is the enslaver who inflicts misery on them. Their only crime is the pursuit of freedom. Therefore, my answer to your question is: For those whose only aim is to seek power over you and to enslave you and your loved ones, for them your precious life is nothing but a worm-like existence they trash under their heels. That's when humans become inhuman - barbarians."

Eustafan's life spans centuries, he is a crusader for liberty and justice, an apostle who was imprisoned for life, executed and resurrected, blindfolded and given up for dead, tortured and crucified. His tongue was removed from his mouth so he could speak the truth no longer. He is tall and lean. His eyes are kind and his expression considerate. His face is made up of many races. He could be man, woman, child - a multidimensional being chiselled like sculpture in stone. He criss-crossed all the continents encouraging everyone for whom enslavement equals slow death to follow him on his path to a place where dignity is as essential in preserving the human race as breathing or making love. At the end of his long journey he built a House on the Hill in a country where the absence of liberty is unthinkable. It became a sanctuary, a place to reflect on one's life, for all those who bravely cut off the chains to set themselves free. The House on the Hill where Eustafan lives is a modest structure made of stones and bricks with large windowpanes which mirror the red sun as it descends in slow motion towards the horizon. The house overlooks a distant City where during the day a glistering Liberty River meanders through like a giant snake whose head and tail got lost in the impenetrable murkiness of immense infinity. During the night the metropolis explodes in a myriad lights outnumbering and outshining the stars penetrating the dark sky above.

The house has a garden, gallery, music room and library, undivided by walls. From time to time a Silvery Bird flies in through the open window and sprinkles the flowers with water from the Liberty River. The paintings hanging in the gallery are paintings in paintings as if all art is a door inviting us to enter another magnificent gallery. The music room resonates with the spellbinding sound of a tenor saxophone suspended from the ceiling on a string. It turns around like a propeller powered by the gravity of thought. There are as many books in the library as there are spoken languages on the planet. The empty spaces on shelves are reserved for forbidden books.

The prophet's day begins the same way it ends. He reclines in a white rocking chair in a large living room facing the floor-to-ceiling window. It seems he may rock the chair at any moment but he never does. He sits still with his eyes piercing the distance, the clouds and the sky, beyond the darkness of eternity. A stream of visitors arrives - men, women and children. They fill all spaces around him and listen to what he has to say.

One late morning about two dozen visitors gathered in the room. After a long silence Eustafan said: "The majority of human beings never leave their country, city, or village - their sacred place of birth. Some die in the same house and in the same room and in the same bed where for the first time they took their first breath and their eyelids opened. Their hearts would shatter the moment they would have to say good bye to what makes the essence of their existence. It is unimaginable for them have to leave behind the soil, which slipped through their fingers so many times on the graves of their ancestors. For this one and only reason their roots branched into the soil wide and deep. Although mortified with gruesome everyday reality, they choose to be accommodating. They stay forever despite the barbed wire surrounding their homes. Their lives are reduced to nothingness."

I recollected my own experience. The Germans invaded my country when I was a boy. After them the Soviets came to seemingly stay forever. The two occupying forces brought with them their language, culture and well-developed plans for the future mental and physical extermination of the nation. The imposition of a foreign ideology (vis-à-vis German & Soviet Marxist-Leninism) further bolstered by local propagandists (collaborators) created an atmosphere of ever present fear. At first the beleaguered population tries to elude their new class of guardians by pretending compliance. But in the end as the mechanism of oppression increases in cruelty, they succumb. In the end, accepting the circumstances as unavoidable fate, they obey the rules of their enslavers in exchange for a chance to continue living. But deep inside, the same way a hungry and thirsty person has no greater longing than for a crumb of bread and a drop of water, many captives of subjugation have no greater longing than to climb the mountain, swim the river and cut the barbed wire with their teeth to reach freedom.

But the many who stay behind face a bleak future. With a heavy padlock on their lips, from morning till night they face a wall defaced with deceitful slogans. They are only allowed to speak with permission from a Guard determined to change their habits. He carries the key to the padlock in his pocket everywhere he goes. He acts like a snake in the grass, carefully concealing his own address and making sure his telephone number is unlisted. But whenever he feels like it, he appears without notice. After he bangs on their door he expects that they will obey his orders at the snap of his fingers.

This kind of submission can break the heart of someone lacking the strength to endure these wrongs. He falls from psychic exhaustion right where he's standing. Others go insane. But then there are those who one day wake up knowing they have only one life to live. It cannot be repeated. They attempt the impossible out of desperation. At an unsuspecting moment they seize the key to the padlock from the Guard – and nobody ever sees them again. Thus they become refugees who settle down in an unknown world in an unknown place. They spread out on both banks of the Liberty River. On a hill above them,

Eustafan's house shines like a beacon in the night. And when they come for a visit, Eustafan greets them:"You're brave and you're courageous and from now on your mind is free and your body is no longer shackled!"

The other day a father with two children entered the room. The boy was about nine and his sister seven. Eustafan pointed to them. He said: "You are my son and you are my daughter, your Father is my brother and your Mother is my sister."

All of a sudden the Silvery Bird flew in and out. The boy asked: "Why is the bird so restless?"

"Because only birds and thoughts have their wings in constant motion," responded Eustafan. "

And when the little girl touched his white rocking chair and inquired: "Why don't you rock?", he answered: "Because it is easy to rock in something that is rock able but to rock in something that is not rock able is almost an impossible task. In other words: it is easy to say something where you are free to say it but it is impossible to say it where for saying it your tongue will be extracted from your mouth as a warning to others."

When the Father asked: Is there a certain set of rules for humans to understand their existence?" Eustafan reached for a book he kept nearby and opened it. The pages were yellow and the print fading with time. He called it Jasper and read: "Man realizes his existence through a free act, that he can be only his actual existence, and hence that his existence eludes objective understanding. These are in fact assertions about the existential act, instances of knowledge. It is no objection to observe that a man does not exist merely as a given thing and that his minimal free existence does not assure his complete human perfection. Certain situations serve to bring man's efforts at achieving autonomy to an abrupt and tragic halt. These are the fundamental limit-situations , which bring man to sudden awareness of his dependent, transient nature, the inadequacy of the empirical mode of being, and the ordination of existence to transcendence. Among these situations are man's condition as a mortal, suffering, and sinful being, together with his sense of historical decisiveness and fidelity, his absolute power of free action, and his need for communication with others. These limit-situations are, at the same time, the sure indices of our possible existence."

The most peculiar of the paintings in The House on the Hill is called The Evocation of Lenin. Salvator Dali made it in 1931. Roughly half a room is depicted in the painting that measures about 90cm x 120 cm. The dominating feature is a thin man clad in black with a white beard who sits in the left lower corner on a black box with his body turned at such an angle that his face cannot be seen. His right hand rests on the backrest of a carved chair. Its seat is covered with a green cloth on which 16 red cherries are found. Two-thirds of this strangely composed work is taken up by an open concert grand. From his position, the man is undoubtedly absorbed in watching the keys. Six golden halos are spread across it at even intervals. They illuminate six Lenin heads. They progress in perspective from the smallest to the largest – from the bass to treble clef. On the white paper above them, instead of notes, there are sixteen ants running about in frenzy.

Despite all attempts at an objective evaluation, Dali's message, as is usually the case with his work, is not altogether clear. The idea could be nothing more than the artist's choice of who or what he feels at the moment is the object of general interest on history's stage. Each surreal element within bears a horror that is all the more appalling when projected by time's projector from a work of art to our naivety. But one thing is clear: We should not see gods in tyrants but at times of great despair subject them to the humiliation of parody.

When asked about the meaning of the painting Eustafan said:" The other way and to me the only way to explain our existence - instead of philosophizing - is through the creation of Art. Those who are not gifted in creating Art, only in perceiving it, as long as they allow the creative process to absorb them wholly, know best about their existence. Religion, political structure, government, business and military - to name a few establishments, which rule our world - cannot compete with the magnitude of Art's immortality. Therefore, to answer your question about the painting's meaning my answer is this: imagine yourself part of the painting and join the man in a black suit looking outward resting his hand on the chair's backrest and ask him what he thinks about the cherries, ants and six Lenin heads placed on the piano keyboard. I can hear him saying: I am waiting for someone to come and since you are now here we can wait together to see what will happen and only when it happens will we know what it is because without a happening the only thing we know is that we have to wait."

Eustafan hands me a pair of binoculars as if his words are to be supported by what I will see. People resembling porcelain dolls walk streets that intersect at a busy crossway. Fifth Avenue intersects Eighth at the place where a fire brought two apartment buildings down yesterday evening. A couple embrace on the sidewalk where Eleventh crosses Fourteenth. Somewhere in its lower north-eastern third it forms a U-turn and intersects the same street a few blocks to the southwest. Above the bustle and romantic idyll, Eustafan's Silvery Bird peacefully circles. And then I freeze: right in the middle of Sixth Avenue a man in black was sitting on a black box staring at the piano - evidently waiting for something to happen.

Quite often the House on the Hill buzzes like a beehive. Eustafan first patiently listens to his visitors. Then he provides them with words of courage: "We, the sailors lost in a fog at sea, strain our eyes to find the lighthouse on the shore. The most important thing in all our actions is that we believe in ourselves. Do in life what you were destined to do. Don't be afraid to exhibit all of your talent. Jump high if you have the strength in your legs and resilient will to exceed your own height."

Just as the blind scream when they see; just as the deaf kneel when they hear; and just as the crippled cast away their crutches and rise the moment they are healed, it is as if fugitives are released from the grasp of boundless tyranny by Eustafan's liberating words. They raise their heads. Their eyes shine. For the first time in their lives they feel as if they're birds learning to fly. Their thoughts grow wings. Each of their stories blends into one and the same: there is no greater reward in a person's life than to be a respected holder of the right to decide his own fate. As soon as this wears away due to one's own negligence or is forcefully removed, life no longer belongs to us but to those to whom we sold it or to whom we have relinquished it without a fight.

The more I look at Eustafan, the more I admire him. My whiteness in comparison with his ebony blackness is almost downright offensive. My freckled arms compared to his sinewy arms are like two bent toothpicks. My brain dulled by mental deprivation is in comparison with the magic of his thinking process, just a dried seed rattling around in a fruit pit. The kindness and wisdom that emanates from him is balsam on the fugitives' aching souls. Many of them, worn out from the long trip, hardly speak, then fall asleep. "There's nothing more touching," Eustafan points out, "than to see a dreamy smile on the tear-soaked face of a sleeping outcast disinherited from his homeland."

Like butterflies to a flower, some converge on the House on the Hill to bid Eustafan farewell. They only have a few hours left and won't live to see tomorrow. They usually seat themselves by the window so they can view in peace the Silvery Bird circling the land. Most of them were born at the onset of the 20th century. During their lives nothing has changed in the ancient law of an eye for an eye, a tooth for a tooth. The dream of utopia as an ideal state in a New World order, in which people joined hands and could without fear dance together in the blossoming meadow, was never fulfilled. Despite the fact that music played all day on the radio, it was only a sound curtain for the lecherous orgies of the power elite – the new-age nobility.

The nationalized voices of the ideology-soaked announcers ceaselessly urge all to dance regardless of whether or not the dancers have the slightest reason to celebrate. This kind of unjustifiable dance with a loveless lover is nothing more than a masquerade ball organized by the state in which the participants make themselves up to look like normalized prostitutes. For this feudalism (in contrast to the preceding feudalism) the stable boy and milkmaid, waking with the sun in a country controlled by members of the IC(ts)O, must pay a hefty tax for permission for their degraded survival: they must dance without knowing why; must remain silent when they want to speak; must harvest the crop so the nobility can carry on with their debauchery, only to throw the people a few crumbs.

The French nobility and slaveholders, aristocrats and feudal lords, the bourgeoisie and squires, the hangmen and torturers over the past hundreds and thousands of years are rolling over in their graves disgusted by the appalling activities of these new-age rulers motivated by the vision of communism as a handy tool in their obsessive pursuit of solidifying their own power.

Yet the game of master and abased, of announcer and dancer, of speaker and silenced, of the rapist and the raped, cannot go on forever unpunished. This game will end as soon as the abased cease to listen, the dancer ceases dancing, the silenced one screams and the lover curses to the grave her impotent lover. This is the moment in which many of Eustafan's visitors, despite having death at the doorstep, overpowered by memories, shake a fist through the room's window at the interminable distance. "Pity all, who like us, the dying, have wasted and continue to waste their lives waiting for a miracle. At least let our dearly-bought experience help those who hope for a just world. May they never lay down their arms!"

There remains the question, however, of how many of those

understand the urgency of such an appeal. Many have not only lost their courage and will to raise arms and fight against evil and injustice, but have also ceased to defend themselves, even if by merely lifting their head. Instead of stomping on the slimy snake and throwing it into the pit, their indolence, apathy and premature defeatism allow the slimy snake to wrap itself around them until they fall gasping for breath.

Then all of a sudden, as if Eustafan's hand were a magic wand, a man appeared as if from nowhere, supporting himself with an apostle's staff so he could stand up straight. He introduced himself as a nameless Arab. He was dressed in white and his eyes glowed with passion. His face emitted an aura, like Eustafan's, as if he'd known, experienced, seen and heard everything. He was always only where he found himself at the moment. Right from the start he said the present cannot be understood without understanding the past, which then opens the door into the future. The past, as he put it, is a sealed box to which we bury once and for all our hope to come to terms with fleeting time and the space surrounding us. A persistent thought twined around the centre of his contemplations like fishing line: if we could anticipate what life has in store for us in the next moment, in the next hour or next day, fate's most guarded secret would be unveiled. Our lives would then lie before us like shell-less turtles. If our lives presently bring to mind a helmless ship, tossed in a stormy sea, how would we act if we knew for certain what awaits us tomorrow? Wouldn't we be better off letting faith in our own immortality guide us?

Darkness began to fall outside. The nameless Arab disappeared as he appeared and the soothing sound of Coleman Hawkins's tenor saxophone slowly filled the room. Eustafan sat facing the window and his soft voice took over where the magic visitor had left his thoughts. Only someone closely bonded with his cultural past, only someone emitting everything good from within and returning humbly to nature, only a person taking care of nature as if it is something very precious, merges lovingly with the forest floor like a fallen pine needle - only this person provides hope that humanity will survive. It won't be easy: for what a strange, bewildering, devastating and blessed world we live in! If yesterday a normal shot from a pistol was still enough to cut down a human being in instinctive motion, today it takes a round from a machine gun to bring a person down. It seems as if our children are going to be far more resilient than we adults. When a terrorist's grenade blows off an arm, a piece of stomach or blasts a hole in his skull, that promising and hardened child, our little ball of sunshine, will run proudly home to show his parents how the nerves are still twitching in the part of the body separated by the blast. At that moment the flapping of wings could be heard as the Silvery Bird flew in through the window and rested on Eustafan's right shoulder. Thousands of lights the size of pinheads quivered in the valley below. A train wheezed in the distance. Its whistle stretched out into the hollow universe. The view was like a painting hanging outside on a thread from the sky itself, shining alone in the night: Some people, apparently pilgrims possessing a vision of their unique existence, pressed side by side on the bank of a wide and muddy river, motionlessly watch a swaying ferryboat approach. At the stern, the white-haired ferryman effortlessly holds the course.

Then I rose, and when I pressed my lips on Eustafan's forehead in farewell, the Silvery Bird caressed my face with its velvety wings. Eustafan accompanied me to the door, grasped my hand in his and said: "When life is at stake, and often even when it's not, I hate verbosity and pseudo-philosophy, empty words and sentences twisted so no one understands them… thus, when life struggles with death, and sometimes it can be a matter of merely gauging their strength, I oppose the kind of Art, which circles around the truth or falsifies it, instead of making the truth available to all suffocated by lies.

On my way home, I kept thinking of those who will never gaspingly make their way to the imaginary House on the Hill, will never knock excitedly on its door and will never sit in Eustafan's room. It's not so long ago that we called our friends by their first names, shook their hands and disentangled our almost invisible presence from their destiny. Surrounded by the night of a foreign land, we bid farewell to them at a distance. In contrast to us, they persevere right where they are, under the most unbearable circumstances. They have our admiration, they have our sympathies. They continue to work and live where they were born. Just as their frustrated days culminate in a pile of festering muck, they are the submissive and enslaved majority. In contrast, we the so-called forgotten handful of pilgrims making our way to the dream House on the Hill, will probably never return. For the time being, we have become the free, unbound minority.

Since the beginning of time, a slice of bread and drop of water are the most tantalizing utopias for those living in poverty and constant misery. But many prefer to die of hunger and thirst than to allow the wings of their ideas to be clipped. The visionaries, from whose lips the words freedom, equality and brotherhood were torn and the lips themselves padlocked, say it is possible to die from hunger and thirst, but a person living in submission, even with a full stomach and pitcher of water in his hands, is dying in the most repulsive corner of the slaveholder's rubbish heap. He becomes a despicable and nameless piece of nothing. The Song of Freedom will never again descend to his scourged mind. Never again will he hear the sounds of the rare and beloved music of Coleman Hawkins. Drained of his strength, still breathing but not free, he slowly disappears into obscurity without a trace.

VII. JAZZ CONNECTIONS

If Coleman Hawkins'
tenor sax interpretation
of **Body and Soul**
is an unforgettable poem –
Charlie Parker on the alto
is the Johann Sebastian Bach
of the 20th century

When you play jazz, you cannot lie.
Sidney Bechet

A blatant lie (in contrast to the truth we experience in listening to beloved music) creeps through the dank catacombs of a life without freedom. A lie slides down the face of a decent person in the form of spit. He wipes it away with his sleeve when possible. But the saliva running down does not bother some. They become willing participants in a sado-masochistic orgy of submission. Setting aside the unique character of their inherent individuality, the subordinate individual who positions his face to be spit on is like a fly that enjoys being trapped in a spider web. To be spat on by the vile slaveholder, he prolongs his bare existence from one hour to the next. The insatiable spider toys with him until his death.

The state of subordination suits those incapable of imagining a life other than that of subordination. Some even praise the ruler claiming his iron fist prevents anarchy. At the same time, in the corner of their withering little souls they snicker at how they have outwitted the spitters with fox-like slyness. At least for now they have secured a warm dinner. The slaveholder's lie is far more acceptable than death by hanging in the name of some intangible truth. The spat-on slave forgets that most massacres have resulted from lies publicly approved by the masses, gathered on a city square. As a result the same masses, turned into foot soldiers by the lying enslaver, never returned home from the pogroms they shouted for.

No other ideological and political set-up has attracted as flypaper to its sticky strip, so many opportunists as Marx & Engels Communist Manifesto (1848). The self-proclaimed apostles of the proletariat, the members of the International Communist (terrorist and subversive) Organization, quickly spotted in the work of these bourgeois theoreticians the most sacred of their ten commandments. The first commandment is to unabashedly live off the labour of a diligent person. With the pretence of constructing a classless future - the worker's paradise - they induct themselves as new-age slaveholders.

There's nothing sadder than seeing a subservient individual. He obediently joins the rest of the apathetic herd at the sound of a whistle. Squeezing together in severe frost around the heated podium, theyapplaud the speaker's deceitful slogans. With a cheer they urge him to continue his shameless spitting. It is, above all, the anxiety of the enslaved to go on with living and protect his family from hardship that makes him endure anything the tyrant wants. The patronizing lifting of his little finger, or his offer of a bone previously spurned by a dog, are gestures through which our comrade, disguised as an omnipotent lord, pretends to be a self-sacrificing provider.

The communist slave, covered in spittle, wanders through the hostile streets. He doesn't know which way to go. He'll die of sorrow unless an unexpected miracle occurs. Humiliated and ill-fated little soul! There's no dignity in helplessly hanging your head and waiting for miracles beneath a window from which rises an exultant jazz solo by a black musician, a free man.

Just as in the past, today's relationships among people consist of a continuous succession of attempts by the stronger to rule the weaker. It's not about physical strength, but about cynical deception on the one side and the servant's gullibility on the other. Archaeologists, examining the tombs of those who refused to yield, find ample proof of this systematic effort to rule one's fellowman. Historians have discovered slaves' messages written in blood on the walls of slave ships. Gravediggers speak about horrible wounds on the bodies (and souls) of innocent prisoners sentenced to die. The mountains echo with cries of citizens murdered in slaughterhouses for their dissent. Never forget, communist enslavers! Listen attentively to what you hear! Blues is music from the hearts of black Africans. They slaved in the sweltering heat on American plantations without any hope that their fate would change. Their music speaks of sadness, but above all of unfailing longing for freedom. In the end they did become free and so will the new-age slaves - one day the spirit of jazz will bring down the prison wall you've built.

Life experiences so arduously gained at present are life experiences gained at the same cost in the past. To understand the past and to derive a lesson from it is the most basic obligation of each individual. Without understanding the past, the reason for defeat and victory, it is almost inevitable that a new enslavement will occur. What a pity that the generation dying away fails to pass on to the ensuing generation its obtained knowledge in the form of a comprehensive, eternally valid and thus completed work. The inability of man to shape the world into a perfect definitive form, in which wisdom once and for all prevails over stupidity, Samaritan virtues over violence, in which justice eliminates injustice and truth overcomes lies

– in short, when good wins out over evil is humanity's bitter failure.

The less attentive the person, the thornier his path. There are those who need to personally experience a car crash to know what it is. Others need the roof over their heads to go up in flames before they understand how destructive a fire is. Some people aren't blind, and yet they can't see; they aren't deaf, and yet they don't perceive any sound, scream or shot. Some even have their heads on the executioner's block, still insisting that the head isn't theirs. People have never before been flooded with such much of detailed information. Literally every tremor within the human body has already been mapped. The beating heart has been extracted from the human torso countless times. Every muscle, nerve, vein and piece of brain tissue has been systematically examined. Every event has been analyzed from all possible aspects, angles and in the bloodiest colours. Intricate waves of radio and television stations encircle the globe like a fishing net. Nothing remains hidden from us. And it's for this very reason that the dismissal of obvious facts, which predetermine the direction of future events, lead to irremediable damage.

If an individual, an eye-witness of the times, pleads ignorance by saying that he doesn't understand how to view things, that he can't tell the difference between truth and lies, that he doesn't comprehend what he sees and hears, doesn't know who his friends and enemies are and which side to join if a crucial fight takes place, then there's nothing left to do but wish him the best of luck on his path to self-destruction. With such indifference, these people dig their own deep ditch into which they'll eventually fall. The careless oversight of galling events, the turning of a blind eye to the torture of one's fellowman and the uncommitted stance at the conduct of the new-age slaveholders are all nothing more than the well-considered actions of a sly Philistine. These intentionally unaware Philistines, turned into apathetic and submissive masses, slyly carry out every tyrant's wish - to preserve their status quo.

Just as a calf is sometimes born with six feet, two heads or without a fully developed brain, a fair number of humans with mental abnormalities are coming into this world. They are the future members of the IC (ts) O - the new-age enslavers. Whoever feels there is lots of time to end the tyranny of these monsters will run into a wall. Ill-fated slave of the contemporary world act now! The International Communist (terrorist and subversive) Organization is amassing at its core power-hungry sub-normals, who are tirelessly building this wall around you. They are not about to give up their criminal intentions unless you yourself challenge them to a life-or-death fight and destroy the hated barriers with your own hands!

The intercourse of amorality with a perverse state gives birth to an immense lie – the source of all communist acts. Inverted morals and a perverse state elevated to the level of normalcy are the basic attributes of the process of enslavement. We witness their revolting world, which has created an endless string of dreaded situations - neighbour fearing neighbour, a mother her own daughter and a commonly known murderer becoming the chairperson of the socialist jury. The amoral way communists regard the basic living needs of a decent person (including his petty dreams and pious wishes) allows for bankrupt existences, so that within the revolutionary justification of their acts they can confiscate the biggest piece of cake. By disseminating fear, they rule over the citizen who shuts his eyes instead of investigating the cause of events happening around him. He overlooks the fact that zealots engage in a revolution for the advantages that the revolution yields them.

Those who are vile and shifty, as well as crafty and spineless can then, within the framework of their self-made laws, dump their accumulated wrath on the backs of the non-revolutionary class enemy. They push forward on the internationally coordinated path to their indefinable goal: total debasement. By undermining a person's faith in the values he has always believed in, by trashing his spirituality, dominion can be achieved over a society burdened with uncertainty. Disorderliness must first, however, be kindled. Only in the thoughts of the most barbaric impostor – the left-wing intellectual, member of the working-class "nobility" and demagogue of the ultra-new communist bureaucracy – can there arise the idea of the total debasement of the results of thousands of years of mankind's efforts. A pyramid office complex with a dirty staircase to a comrade's revolutionary preserve can never replace a precious cathedral, the pearl of centuries past. A propaganda newspaper can never be considered a sacred testament as can an ancient copy of the Bible. Machine-gun fire cannot substitute for a majestic symphony. A psychopath's crack of a whip cannot replace the thoughts of a prudent person or a meaningful life.

Criminals disguised as lovers of the underprivileged carry out the total debasement of all proven values, to which man has advanced with ant-like diligence. In fact, amorality and perversion is their calling card. They surround their corrupt lives with fortresses, from which they emerge with pomp and fanfare. The left-wing intellectual, working-class "nobility" and demagogue of the ultra-new communist bureaucracy – comrade apparatchiks – have blended under the lag of an international alliance. All across the globe they play despotic games with millions of human lives.

The actions of the Italian IC(tp)O and French IC(tp)O are telling examples. Both of these organizations have attracted a significant number of followers (many of them renowned intellectuals) to the idea of the minority's victory over the majority through cooperation within the framework of a so-called historical compromise. This cooperation is based on the notion that the majority will be allotted a minority role. Then at an opportune time, the minoritized majority will be stripped of all its crucial rights, and banished with a laugh to pastures among mooing cows.

The propelling force behind this revolutionary elite – the left-wing intellectual, working-class "nobility" and demagogue of the ultra-new communist bureaucracy – is a credo deeply rooted in the depths of their communist soul: it isn't in a moron's nature to label his life as moronic and his revolutionary work as wasted time.

The archenemy stands before the gate of the hitherto free world and patiently watches. He can't wait until the hen squawking beyond the walls of this hated kingdom lays the long-awaited egg. This rotten egg is essentially a time bomb, smuggled behind the Iron Curtain by revolutionary maniacs like the wooden horse into Troy. As soon as the clock ticks down to the appointed hour, the rotten egg will emerge. When the shell bursts upon impact with the pavement - our terrorist-besieger will have won. A debasing stench, which turns everything upside down, will begin to spread through the hitherto unconquered area of the free world. The sky, until recently clear blue, changes into hell, freedom into a vehement poison, happiness into an unnecessarily taxing feeling, self-confidence into depression and sense into nonsense. In other words, there will no longer be anything to live for. There has yet to be a genius in the field of transforming the world in his own image who has come up with a better way, without a destructive war, of pinning his opponent on his back and depriving him of that which is dearest to him - freedom.

The final aim of the Worldwide Socialist Revolution, whose concluding phase is communism, is not to create the conditions enabling a dignified person to live in dignity, so that a worker can be proud of his work, the poet can celebrate beauty, the inventor create successful inventions for humanity, the farmer gaze out with satisfaction over his rich crop or the teacher straighten the backbones of children made crooked by the falseness of the adult world. Instead, the privileged handful of slackers, international adventurers and debasers of everything spiritual, in the name of the World Socialist Revolution, dream about expanding their domain over free nations. Their aim is to divide among themselves their material assets. On one hand, the more intelligent, gifted, skillful and, especially, free the people, the higher is their standard of living. On the other hand, in countries squeezed tight by the belt of a communist dictator, the worker's pursuit of a crumb of bread is another opportunity for the state provider - the owner of all bakeries - to sneer at his subject and make him even more degradingly dependent on the crumb of bread dropped at his doorstep.

Disgraced and nationalized participant of an ideological system never before so corrupted! Tear down the palaces of these narcissistic bureaucrats, cut the barbed wire, and speak your decisive NO to the intellectual eunuch, who is unjustifiably deciding your present and future. Cry YES to the alto saxophonist Charlie Parker. What you hear are his unrestrained bebop cascades. It's a voice arising from absolute freedom, the voice of jazz music.

It is the primary obligation of each individual and of society, with a strong enough will to remain free, to maintain an interest in the unadulterated values of the past. It is necessary to keep pace with current events and prepare a fertile soil void of sham and lies for the next generation. In contrast, in countries controlled by the IC(tp)O, we can only speak of a distorted past, gutted and cut up into pieces. A pyramid best characterizes current events. Its base is supported on the shoulders of moaning serfs. As for the future, those who keep in mind one of the most important tips will best resist: a black jazz saxophonist's improvisation is symbolic speech, a musical legacy of former African slaves, who would today rather die than allow themselves to be enslaved again tomorrow. For whoever plays jazz speaks the truth. Remember well, tyrant! You never silence the musician by stripping him of his instrument. Music will find you everywhere, even in the furthest corner. And there, your kind will justly disintegrate into dust and nothingness!

VIII. Quo usque tandem?

a) The earth's land and the entire population presently inhabiting this land, i.e. the entire world, is divided into two parts:

I. The part controlled by members of the International Communist (terrorist and subversive) Organization.[1]

II. The second part is so far the free world.

[1] *The People's Republic of China is a concentration camp with the largest number of politically unwanted* prisoners in the world. The USSR is the largest concentration camp in the world with regard to land size. By joining these two concentration camps in the near future, a single concentration camp will be formed with the following parameters: the largest number of politically unwanted* prisoners will be found on the world's largest expanse of land.*

*unwanted = a prisoner with no chance of surviving

b) The cultural, social, economic and political situation, i.e. the quality of life for not only each individual, but also the entire society, nation or state, exists in this basic division of the world – the one subjugated and the other free – and is directly and proportionately affected by it. Each day of the year, each hour in this day and each minute in this hour there occurs on our planet a further redistribution of the population and territory.

c) Every day, hour and minute new territories and a large group of the free population come, imperceptibly as it were, under control of the International Communist (terrorist and subversive) Organization.

d) Each day, hour and minute is thus for a free person an hour or minute irrevocably decisive.

e) At the very moment that new territory and populations come under control of the IC(ts)O, the thought of turning around is an absurd dream of the ensnared in an inhuman trap. There is no turning back.

f) The systematic redistribution of territory and of the population living on it is the result of the terrorist and subversive efforts of the IC(ts)O.

g) The headquarters of this organization is the Union of Soviet Socialist Republics.

h) The USSR is a terrorist and subversive state that doesn't hesitate to use whatever means or methods necessary to achieve its goals. This goal is to rule the world.

i) The IC(ts)O with its headquarters in Moscow absorbs new territories and populations by way of intensive terrorist and subversive activities at a seemingly gradual pace. It accomplishes this through small, inconspicuous wars. As it turns out, these small, local wars (mini-revolutions) to weaken the free world are entirely sufficient. One after another after another, like falling dominoes, they represent an all-or-nothing fight. As soon as the physically and morally exhausted free world hangs its head, it will be gagged and bound.

j) The free world will be physically and morally weakened when each free individual loses interest in the circumstances that arise from the loss of his own unique and unrepeatable freedom. A human being loses interest in these circumstances when he begins to struggle for his dear life. The fight for one's dear life is an act of desperation. The desperate person then crawls on all fours to the nearest street corner to accept from someone's outstretched hand a handful of rice.

k) A human being can be manipulated into this kind of humiliating submission when he is physically and morally broken, and saving his own dear life is the sole thing he clings to.

l) The population of the hitherto free world must never allow the attempt to stay alive at all costs to completely paralyse its thinking. As soon as one allows the will to survive to gain prevalence over the will to live freely, he can count on that handful of rice at the street corner, crawled to with the last of his strength, to be his last meal on the way to a burning hell. The moment a free person accepts this handful of rice and stuffs it into his mouth, he becomes a slave: he himself and the land he lives on become the irrevocable property of the communist slaveholder.

m) A free human being, who does not wish to live at all costs and anyway cannot do so, will never crawl to the street corner for a handful of rice and heroically sacrifices his free life in the fight against the communist usurpers.

n) The free world and people who have until now inhabited the free world's territory will never have to fight for their lives if they realize in time that they're living through a historically decisive day, hour and unrepeatable minute. Then it's enough just to declare the enemy the sole archenemy – the communist usurper – and act accordingly.

***

If a human being complacently accepts, as his sole life alternative, participation in the unprincipled system of a classless society, in which only the elite slaveholders rule slaves stripped of all identity; if a person does not occupy on principle a negative position toward the ultimatum of the hierarchy of new-age political super-cops, demanding that life be lived under conditions in which morality is inverted and the perversely pathological state is elevated to the state of normalcy; if we all are to passively watch the demagogic attempts of the crooked revolutionary to introduce a worldwide dictatorship of the proletariat, in which the honest and noble worker won't play the slightest role; if the hitherto free person, whose moral and sacred obligation is to safeguard the world from its otherwise unavoidable end, does not deal a mortal blow to its archenemy – the IC(tp)O – and does not flush this enemy away; if the devoted gendarme of their new-age genocide, the Union of Soviet Socialist Republics, is not pushed back to its place behind the Iron Curtain in time, enclosing it to experiment on members of its own communist super race in its own ruined country it will continue to develop its own psychopathic ideology. Unless we immediately treat these and other terrorist and subversive states as terrorist and subversive states, meaning that unless all bridges between them and us are demolished, all access roads are blocked and all doors and back entrances are nailed shut and if the hitherto free man pays little attention to this obvious raping and choking of the world, and does not destroy his archenemy right away - then he may find that any decision tomorrow will be too late.

So long as a free and therefore vulnerable person sits around at home lulled to sleep by the tapping of a blossoming magnolia branch on the glass pane of his half-opened window; so long as the wax from a burning motley-colored candle placed on the piano top continues to drop and the flame flickers with each touch of a key by deft fingers of the beautiful daughter; so long as the radio commentator's remark that in order to avoid having all of our descendents die in the near future for their country it is absolutely necessary for each of our fifth sons to die now, is viewed as nonsense by logically and prudently thinking parents; so long as we see on the screen of the greenish bluish red television on 24 channels, 24 hours a day, Walt Disney's delightful animals charmingly imitating all our bad habits; so long as the overstocked refrigerator purrs like a kitten and our food contains the scientifically recommended number of calories; so long as there are pine logs burning in the fireplace and we're warm and well; so long as the sun shines at least an hour a day, seven hours a week and the grass is green, the tangerines are orange and bananas yellow; so long as our children aren't terrorized in their sleep by:

1. Snow-white with her eye gouged out by the laser ray of an anti-missile gun,

2. Sleeping Beauty put to sleep forever by radioactive fallout from the 1,125th experimental explosion by the Peking-Kremlin peacefully antagonistic neo-colonizers,

3. The head of Robinson Crusoe speared on the bayonet of a Red Guardsman.

4. The bejewelled ghost under a translucent robe has her left breast shot off by the malicious Hitler youth of North Korea –

So long as all of this can be true (and then again it doesn't have to be); so long as we can play around for fun with our own dreams and horrific ideas and push them as need be into dark corners; so long as the blossoming magnolia branch does not for some reason suddenly stop tapping on the window; so long as someone does not tear from the placid reader's hand the book he is currently reading by H. Stuckenschmidt – Twentieth Century Music – and does not throw it into the fireplace's blaze; so long as these strangers – suddenly appearing from nowhere and perfectly organized in liquidation teams – do not shove us out into the cold and do not kick in our beautiful white teeth with their steel-toed boots; so long as they don't begin to preach, with a megaphone amplifying a corrupted voice 100 times, passages from a novel of the Soviet laureate of the International Lenin Prize for Strengthening Peace Among Nations; so long as we aren't asked obtrusive questions on which activities we were involved in, let's say, 35 years ago, why we're alive instead of happily committing suicide; so long as all sacred paintings, including The Last Supper aren't ripped out by sharpened scythes; so long as the statue of the Czech duke and knight Wenceslas, depicted riding his horse in front of the National Museum in Prague, is not pounded into dust and ashes by sledge hammers; so long as violins don't fly through the air and shatter on the stone pavement of Trafalgar Square – as well as, of course, violas and saxophones, oboes and cymbals and the trumpets of Dizzy Gillespie and numerous other jazz geniuses - so long as the sense and legacy of Marx & Engels Communist Manifesto (1848) and the Great October Socialist Revolution (1917) are not fulfilled by these and other even more demented acts; so long as the archenemy – the cherry-faced communist (just yesterday still referred to as a pinko bastard by everyone) – does not suddenly appear grinning ear to ear before the very eyes of the free and doubting person – that is to say, so long as all of this does not happen, and not until all of this actually happens, will we say goodbye to freedom and life and helplessly ask why we didn't do everything we could to prevent this day from coming – our day of ruin.

***

A phantom is circling the world – the revolutionary ghoul of the communist slaveholder. The earth it has already raped is proof of its destructive paths. Sweepers and washerwomen, milkmaids and shoemakers, masons and farmers, miners and scientists, postmen and clerks, salespeople and seamstresses, tinsmiths and toolmakers, teachers and concrete workers, dentists and firefighters, electricians and guitarists, engineers and switchmen, children and the elderly all have the same solitary question in their sleepy eyes: How much longer?

Workers!
Honest and noble citizens of the whole world!
Don't let anyone enslave you!
Don't let anyone take away your right to become the master of your unique and unrepeatable life!

Ottawa (1975)

Epilogue

Jiří TAUFER

An excerpt from the text on a book flap:

Each book we publish and will publish in the future is a weapon for our socialist people to use in the fight with the remnants of the old capitalist society in the minds of the reader, in his fight with nature, in the fight for socialism, for peace and for communism.

SVOBODA (LIBERTY) publishing house

Prague (1975)

Jiří Klobouk
Anti-Communist Manifesto
1975
A Period Document